DATE DUE

NO 4 '02			
DE 8 '07			

DEMCO 38-296

ASPECTS OF MONOTHEISM

—HOW GOD IS ONE—

On the cover: Michelangelo's *Separation of Light from Darkness* is the first of nine biblical scenes on the Sistine Chapel ceiling, a flattened barrel vault more than 130 feet long. Between 1508 and 1512, Michelangelo made hundreds of preparatory drawings and then painted the frescoes in reverse chronological order, beginning with the *Drunkenness of Noah* and ending with God's creation of the world. Appropriately, this first (but last-painted) fresco in the series illustrates verses 3-4 of the opening chapter of Genesis: "Then God said, 'Let there be light'; and there was light. And God saw that light was good; and God separated the light from the darkness." *Photo by Scala/Art Resource, NY.*

Aspects of Monotheism

—HOW GOD IS ONE—

Symposium at the Smithsonian Institution
October 19, 1996

*Sponsored by the
Resident Associate Program*

CONTRIBUTORS

Donald B. Redford
William G. Dever
P. Kyle McCarter, Jr.
John J. Collins

EDITORS

Hershel Shanks
Jack Meinhardt

Biblical Archaeology Society
Washington, DC

Library of Congress Cataloging-in-Publication Data

Aspects of Monotheism: how God is one: symposium at the Smithsonian
Institution, October 19, 1996, sponsored by the Resident Associate
Program/contributors, Donald B. Redford ... [et al.]; editors,
Hershel Shanks, Jack Meinhardt.

p.   cm.

Includes bibliographical references (p.).

ISBN 1-880317-19-2 (hardcover). — ISBN 1-880317-50-8 (pbk.)

1. Monotheism—Middle East—Congresses. 2. Monotheism—Egypt—
Congresses. 3. Monotheism—Biblical teaching—Congresses.
4. Bible —Antiquities—Congresses. 5. Middle East—Antiquities—
Congresses. 6. Egypt—Antiquities—Congresses. 7. Middle East—
Religion—Congresses. 8. Egypt—Religion—Congresses.
I. Redford, Donald B. II. Shanks, Hershel. III. Meinhardt, Jack, 1956- .

BL1060.A74 1997
291.2′11—dc21   97-34911
CIP

Designed by Sean Kennedy

© 1997 Biblical Archaeology Society
4710 41st Street, NW
Washington, DC 20016

CONTENTS

Participants   6

Introduction   9

The Monotheism of Akhenaten   11
Donald B. Redford

Folk Religion in Early Israel: 27
Did Yahweh Have a Consort?
William G. Dever

The Religious Reforms of Hezekiah and Josiah   57
P. Kyle McCarter, Jr.

Jewish Monotheism and Christian Theology   81
John J. Collins

Color Plates   97

Audience Questions   107

Glossary   121

List of Illustrations   126

Acknowledgments   132

Donald B. Redford is the foremost authority on Akhenaten, often called the world's first monotheist. Professor of Near Eastern Studies at the University of Toronto, Redford has been the director of the Akhenaten Temple Project at the University of Pennsylvania since 1972, which led to his production of a film on the project's findings. Redford's publications include *Egypt, Israel and Canaan in Ancient Times* (Princeton Univ. Press, 1992) and *Akhenaten: The Heretic King* (Princeton Univ. Press, 1984). He is also editor-in-chief of the forthcoming *Oxford Encyclopedia of Ancient Egypt* and has written a libretto for an opera, *Ra*.

William G. Dever is professor of Near Eastern Archaeology and Anthropology at the University of Arizona. He lived for many years in Jerusalem, leading excavations at Gezer from 1966 to 1971 and again in 1984, and he served as director of the William F. Albright School of Archaeological Research in Jerusalem from 1971 to 1975. Dever is the author of numerous articles and books on the archaeology of the biblical period; he is also the senior editor for Israel/Palestine of the *Oxford Encyclopedia of Near Eastern Archaeology* and a principal archaeology advisor for the *Anchor Bible Dictionary*.

P. **Kyle McCarter, Jr.** is the William Foxwell Albright Professor of Biblical and Ancient Near Eastern Studies and chairman of the Near Eastern Studies Department at The Johns Hopkins University. A past president of the American Schools of Oriental Research, he is the author of commentaries on 1 and 2 Samuel in the *Anchor Bible* series. His other writings include contributions to the *Oxford Companion to the Bible*, *Harper's Study Bible* and *Harper's Bible Commentary*. McCarter's most recent book is *Ancient Inscriptions: Voices from the Biblical World* (Biblical Archaeology Society, 1996).

John J. Collins is a professor of Hebrew Bible at the University of Chicago Divinity School. He has served as president of the Catholic Biblical Association and as editor of the *Journal of Biblical Literature*. He is also a member of the expanded team of Dead Sea Scrolls editors. His publications include a commentary on *Daniel* (Fortress Press, 1993), *The Scepter and the Star: The Messiahs of the Dead Sea Scrolls* (Doubleday, 1995), *Apocalypticism in the Dead Sea Scrolls* (Routledge, 1997) and *Seers, Sibyls and Sages in Hellenistic-Roman Judaism* (Brill, 1997).

INTRODUCTION

This is the most exciting, provocative and readily understandable discussion of monotheism in its various aspects that I have seen. Stemming from a symposium at the Smithsonian Institution in Washington, D.C., organized by the Biblical Archaeology Society, *Aspects of Monotheism: How God Is One* presents the rich and variegated views of four distinguished scholars on different facets of what is a rich and variegated concept—the idea of one universal God.

Perhaps some of the excitement is a result of the sensitivity of the subject. Were the ancient Israelites really the first to worship a single god, or did the Egyptians beat them to the punch? And were the ancient Israelites really monotheists, or was the idea of a single, universal God a late development in Israelite history? What can archaeology tell us about the subject? Is it possible that the Israelite god Yahweh had a female consort? Did popular religion in ancient Israel depart from the monotheistic strictures in the Hebrew Bible? And what of Christianity? How are we to understand the divinity of Jesus, alongside his Father? Even more difficult, how are we to understand the Trinity?

The presentations in this book tackle these questions forthrightly and provide some surprising answers. Despite the complex, even philosophical, nature of the subject and the breadth of concrete scholarly materials that bear on it, the authors write in language that is perfectly accessible to the layperson. For that reason, I predict that this book will become standard fare in college courses and adult discussion groups. It will provide the basis for innumerable stimulating conversations. I envy the reader confronting this material for the first time.

Hershel Shanks

THE MONOTHEISM OF AKHENATEN

Donald B. Redford

Monotheism, polytheism and henotheism are constructs of the Judeo-Christian tradition. They manifest a mindset quite different from that of ancient man. These concepts, along with such pejorative categories as heathens, pagans and idolaters, reflect a rationalization of history that seems natural to us but was not characteristic of ancient cultures. The use of such terms assumes a period of ignorance followed by a period of revelation. The revelation is always thought to have occurred in the remote past. How the Supernatural operates in the present, long after the revelation, is never really addressed.

For ancient man, the situation was quite different. For him, the Supernatural never ceased to interact with the human community and the cosmos. There was no great revelation. If there was ever a break between time past and present, it was marked by creation itself: chaos before, order afterwards.

It would never have occurred to an ancient Egyptian to postulate the Supernatural as a monad—a unitary, intellectually superior emanation. Much less would it have occurred to him to suppose that his eternal salvation depended on the recognition of such a monad. One man might choose to worship this god or that; another might even hold, for whatever reason, that other gods did not exist. But this was not important for an ancient Egyptian. He could not have cared less.

An ancient Egyptian would have objected only when some belligerent proselytism threatened to affect the lives of the populace, perhaps by tearing down the old temples and their landed estates or by prohibiting ordinary forms of worship. But even then, his objection would have had nothing to do with how many gods were worshiped.

This can be illustrated by the case of the pharaoh Akhenaten (1352-1336 B.C.E.), who, in modern times, is sometimes called the first monotheist. After Akhenaten's death, Egyptians immediately reverted to their old religious norms. Akhenaten was then labeled a "rebel" and a "doomed one" because he had overthrown the socioeconomic system and had almost disrupted the running of the state. But no one back then ever called him anything like "monotheist" (whatever lexical form that would have conjured up in the Egyptian language), and certainly no pejorative was ever hurled at him for espousing one god.

The Egyptians, like most ancient peoples, experienced the Supernatural as infinite plurality. It impinged upon their lives in multifarious ways, from beneficial to inimical. It consisted of innumerable wills and personalities.

From late prehistoric times, this infinite plurality, this Supernatural, translated itself into a series of gods, powers of heaven and earth, and *numina*—all organized at first on a parochial level as

Pharaoh Amenophis IV took the name Akhenaten (Servant of Aten) when he established his cult of the Sun-disc (the god Aten) at Amarna. Akhenaten has been called the first monotheist, because he conceived of the Sun-disc as the sole god—self-engendered, universal, the creator of all things. This 10-foot-high sandstone statue from Thebes, now in the Cairo Museum, reveals another of Akhenaten's peculiarities: He had himself depicted not as a powerful, imposing monarch but as an effemi-nate figure with rounded hips, an elongated neck and a lantern jaw.

CAIRO MUSEUM

a roster of town gods and later as gods who operated in a wider domain. Clever Roman satirists and epigrammatists like Juvenal and Martial might scoff at the myriad of animal and "kitchen-garden" gods that "demented Egypt" worshiped, but the Egyptians were simply acknowledging that the Supernatural—wherever perceived—interjects itself into the affairs of humanity.

With the advent of the sophisticated pharaonic state in the third millennium B.C.E., the godly pantheon became highly centralized and tightly ranked. Notions of hierarchy and subordination were introduced. Family relationships and specifically assigned functions insinuated themselves into the world of the divine.

That one pre-eminent power should ape the world of men and become King of the Gods was only to be expected. Where he came from was immaterial. That he might team up with solar and chthonic power to become the triune essence of all that exists—the sun, the latent power of the underworld and the earth—is of considerable interest in the evolution of human speculation about the great imponderables. But it is not monotheism!

One unknown Memphite priest, at a remote period of history, perceived the myriad of deities of the Egyptian pantheon as immediate avatars of an underlying One. This One was "in every body, of all living things, animating them by thinking and enunciating [His] will." This is a much more profound break with the past, a true quantum leap as it were; but it is not monotheism either.

Monotheism does not appear through amalgamation and syncretism but rather through the annihilation of other gods. Other divine entities are not simply taken on board and integrated into the pantheon; they are thrown over and left to drown. If they *must* be acknowledged, it is only done by a kind of deconsecration that demotes them to the status of demons and insists that they were never anything else. They are to be destroyed and plastered over. Their worshipers are attacked, and if they cannot be slaughtered like the prophets of Baʿal, they are ridiculed, mocked and vilified.

Most importantly, salvation comes only through an unconditional surrender of intelligence to the Supernatural, who does not need to explain his actions or to reveal himself, except to a single individual.

Small wonder that the three great monotheisms we are familiar with celebrate themselves in hymns larded with military jargon. Small wonder that the Egyptians, when eventually confronted by the faceless, unidentifiable, vindictive Judeo-Christian God, rejected him and declared the religiosity—or irreligiosity—of his fanatical followers *atheism*.

Prior to the Greco-Roman period, the only native Egyptian that we know of who promoted a "one-godism" was Pharaoh Amenophis IV, known as Akhenaten. The expected belligerent streak shows through in his treatment of Amun, the chief god of the Egyptian pantheon. That Akhenaten did not venture on a campaign of forceful proselytism shows only that he did not feel the need: The great Unwashed would follow him blindly since he was their All-in-All. And by the time they realized the folly of Akhenaten's program, he was almost dead anyway.

Akhenaten, the second son of Amenophis III and his royal wife Tiye, was born either towards the end of the 15th century or early in the 14th century B.C.E. These were halcyon days for Egypt and her empire. Amenophis III sat in imperial splendor over all the lands between Karoy in the Sudan and the Euphrates in Mesopotamia, a tract today occupied by all or parts of seven modern states. Amenophis's court became a byword over the known world for its luxury; his reign gave rise to an aristocratic elite such as Egypt had never seen. Amenophis III was proud that his civil service appointments came "from the most elite and the choicest of the whole land." According to an inscription on the Third Pylon of the Temple of Amun at Karnak, Akhenaten congratulated himself: "I did not appoint any who did not have a respectable lineage, reaching back over generations." The art he favored was supercharged with a symbolism expressive of his divinity. He dubbed himself "the Dazzling Sun-disc"—a veritable Louis XIV, *le roi soleil*. The revenues from the empire transformed Egypt into the richest country on earth, a land "in which gold is as plentiful as dust."

Akhenaten succeeded his father and ruled for 17 peaceful years. Despite the prosperity of his reign, following his death there was a general destruction and concealment of his monuments as the populace returned to the old ways. Until recently, however, there has been scarce archaeological or textural material providing information about the pharaoh's reign, or about the man himself.

But now Akhenaten is gradually coming into sharper focus through the careful recovery of bits and pieces of evidence. Three projects in particular are providing this material: the work of the Centre Franco-égyptien in recovering lost relief fragments of Akhenaten's temples from secondary locations where they were used; the renewed British excavations at Tell el-Amarna, Akhenaten's capital, which he called Akhetaten; and my excavation of Akhenaten's earliest temple at Karnak, in Thebes. As a result, the following generalizations can now be made with unassailable conviction:

First, there is no evidence of any co-regency of Akhenaten and his father. Co-regency has in the past been advanced to explain, rather simplistically, the handful of memorials dedicated to Amenophis III at Tell el-Amarna.

Second, there is no evidence of any foreign influence on Akhenaten's revolutionary program of one-godism. Even though his grandfather was Nubian, Akhenaten himself was brought up at the Egyptian capital of Thebes. There is no reason to believe that his wife, Nefertity, was anything but Egyptian. Of his mentors referred to in the records, his uncle served as a priest of the sun god, Aten; his father's vizier was an Egyptian aristocrat; and his childhood tutor was a court flunky who later became Akhenaten's butler. In short, all the ingredients of his "cult" of the Sun-disc—

Egyptian Kings:
Before and After Akhenaten

XVIIIth Dynasty (B.C.E.)

Ahmose	1550-1525
Amenophis I	1525-1504
Thutmose I	1504-1492
Thutmose II	1492-1479
Thutmose III	1479-1425
Hatshepsut	
(co-regent with Thutmose III)	1479-1457
Amenophis II	1427-1400
Thutmose IV	1400-1390
Amenophis III	1390-1352
Amenophis IV (Akhenaten)	**1352-1336**
Smenkhkare	1338-1336
Tutankhamun	1336-1327
Aya	1327-1323
Haremhab	1323-1295

XIXth Dynasty (B.C.E.)

Ramesses I	1295-1294
Seti I	1294-1279
Ramesses II	1279-1213
Merneptah	1213-1203
Seti II	1200-1194
Siptah	1194-1188
Tewosret	1188-1186

the elevation of Aten to supreme and sole god—can be found on Egyptian soil.

Third, although Akhenaten stated that Thebes and its people were uncongenial to him, he nevertheless celebrated a jubilee sometime during his five-year reign there. In Egypt, jubilee festivals, celebrated as far back as the First Dynasty (3100-3000 B.C.E.), sought to reaffirm the legitimacy of the king's reign; both gods and

The crocodile-headed god Sobek (left) extends the sign of life (ankh) *to Pharaoh Amenophis III (1390-1352 B.C.E.), the father of Akhenaten. Unlike his son, Amenophis III worshiped many gods, including Sobek, depicted here in a 9-foot-high alabaster statue, now in the Luxor Museum. The extravagance of Amenophis III's reign is suggested by the 60-foot-high sandstone statues of the pharaoh (opposite)erected in front of his mortuary temple at Thebes. The Romans called these statues the Colossi of Memnon, believing them put up by the mythical king of Ethiopia, Memnon. It was said in antiquity that the northernmost statue (at right) could be heard singing at dawn and dusk—when Memnon greeted and bade farewell to his mother, Eos, the Greek dawn goddess.*

ERICH LESSING

human dignitaries from all over the kingdom were invited to the festival and convened in a great complex of buildings erected specially for the occasion. In connection with his jubilee, Akhenaten erected four large "sun temples" in Thebes. The masonry from Akhenaten's Theban temples was recycled by later generations; between 15 and 20 percent of the relief decoration is still extant in secondary use. By contrast, less than one percent of the original inscriptional material has survived from Amarna (Akhetaten), which served as Akhenaten's capital from his fifth year onwards. It is therefore the earliest period of Akhenaten's reign, his Theban years, that offer the best evidence of the new ideas percolating in his brain.

Fourth, Akhenaten's decision to concentrate his worship on the divine Sun-disc (Aten) cannot be separated, at least in time, from his decision to change the style of Egyptian art. For a brief period at the beginning of the reign, both Aten and the pharaoh himself were depicted in traditional guise; even Amun was allowed to retain his traditional place in the divine iconography. Akhenaten soon modified the artistic canon, however, to accommodate the Sun-disc and its relationship to himself. Above all, Akhenaten had himself represented in a way that, even by the ancients, was not considered flattering: His skull seems malformed, with a lantern-like jaw and an over-heavy head on an elongated neck; and spindly legs support his curiously feminine torso.

One senses that the key to unlocking the mysteries of his reign may lie in our understanding of this peculiar image. Interpretations have veered wildly; some consider him a woman in disguise, while others describe him as a eunuch brought back from the Sudan. Another interpretation is that Akhenaten suffered from a congenital ailment; the chief candidate has been Froehlich's syndrome—but that poses more problems than it solves. The most recent suggestion is that Akhenaten suffered from Marfan's syndrome. The ocular, cardiovascular and musculoskeletal defects of this syndrome indeed match Akhenaten to a T. But this suggestion poses more problems than it solves. In particular, Froehlich's syndrome almost invariably results in early sterility and reduced intelligence; but Akhenaten was neither childless (we know he had at least six daughters) nor mentally challenged.

One school of thought has dismissed physical causes in favor of a symbolic interpretation: Akhenaten decreed that he should be thus depicted simply to convey the idea of himself as an androgynous or hermaphroditic fertility figure—symbolizing the pharaoh's status as father and mother of all mankind. In fact, precisely this kind of androgynous figure does exist in Egyptian art, both before and after Akhenaten, and for this very purpose. If Akhenaten had wanted to depict himself as an androgynous parent of all, he surely would have appropriated the traditional imagery. But, alas, Akhenaten's images look nothing like these other depictions, suggesting that Akhenaten was up to something else.

Fifth and finally, Akhenaten's new program involved the worship of *one* god (the Sun-disc Aten), the graphic and verbal

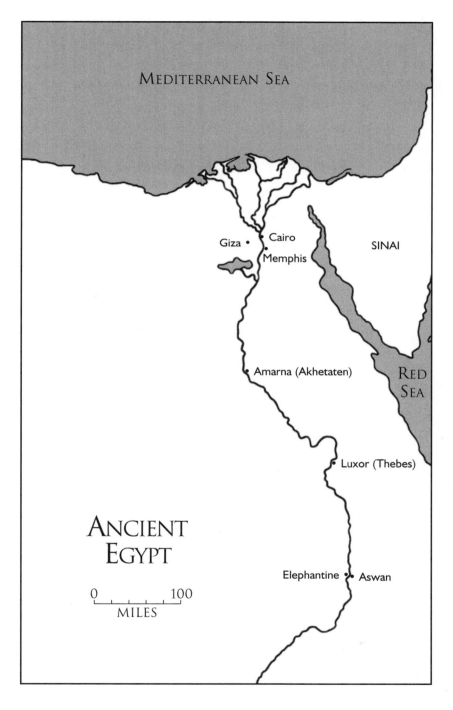

MEDITERRANEAN SEA

Giza •   • Cairo

Memphis

SINAI

Amarna (Akhetaten)

RED
SEA

Luxor (Thebes)

ANCIENT
EGYPT

Elephantine •• Aswan

0   100

MILES

expressions of which were iconoclastic. That is, the traditional use of a ubiquitous, complex symbolism and extended metaphor in describing the Supernatural was given up; even in the minor decorative arts, images smacking of polytheistic symbolism were abandoned.

Some who deny Akhenaten's one-godism have pointed to the occasional use in his royal inscriptions of the word "gods," as well as the divine names Hathor, Shu, Re and Horus, along with Aten. But this argument is specious. Most, if not all, references to these other gods occur very early in Akhenaten's reign, when experimentation was rife, even in the king's own thinking. At that time, sculptors and lector-priests were trying to understand the king's directives, and so tangential interpretations might be expected. The references to Hathor and "the gods" are found in

The Temple of Amun. Amenophis III (whose name means "[the god] Amun is pleased") built the columns in the center of the photograph below as a temple to the chief god of the Egyptian pantheon, Amun. It was here, in Thebes, that Akhenaten was raised; Akhenaten succeeded his father in 1352 B.C.E., ruled from Thebes for five years and then moved his capital to Amarna (Akhetaten).

depictions prepared for the jubilee, which Akhenaten celebrated in his third year and which classically centered upon a conclave of all the gods of Egypt. That the references are exceptional can be shown by the fact that Akhenaten did his best to expunge the gods everywhere in the ritual: The numerous shrines, once filled by the *numina* from Upper and Lower Egypt, were filled by the Sun-disc alone; the hymn to Hathor was bowdlerized to remove all hateful symbolism of the gods. Finally, the solar names Re-harakh Te and Shu appear almost entirely in the new didactic name Akenhaten gave to his new god, and here they have been transmogrified from names into common nouns meaning "sun" and "light": "Live the Sun-Horus of the Horizon, he who rejoices in the horizon in his name of 'Light-which-is-in-the-Sun-disc.'"

The most revealing text about the nature of Akhenaten's new god and his motivation in introducing him is now part of the tenth pylon at Karnak. Although this pylon was erected by Pharaoh Haremhab about a generation after Akhenaten's death, it includes recycled masonry from a gate built by the late heretic and then dismantled. Where the gate originally stood is not clear, but the style of its decoration suggests that it was put up very early in Akhenaten's reign, before his revolutionary art was introduced. Two blocks clearly belonged to a long inscription written in columns. Although 14 columns are partially preserved, neither the first nor the last is extant on the blocks. As a result, not a single complete sentence is preserved either within a column or from column to column. Nonetheless, a progression of thought and content can be discerned.

It is quite striking. The text begins with Akhenaten declaiming that all of the other gods have failed and "ceased" to be effective. But the next few columns of text go further, celebrating another god who has not "ceased." This is a god "[who himself gave birth] to himself, and no one knows the mystery of [...] He [go]es where he pleases and they know not [his] g[oing]." Akhenaten describes his newly adopted god as absolutely unique and located in the heavens. Numerous vignettes, also carved on Akhenaten's dismantled gate, make it clear that the god in question is Re, the Horizon-Horus, or the great sun god. This god is mysterious, celestial and self-engendered, and his creation is exalted.

The inscription on the tenth pylon shows not only that Akhenaten worshiped one god (as we already knew) but that he countenanced the existence of only one god. Column 13 of the inscription gives us a new version of a formula Akhenaten is quite fond of: "How matchless is his god!" Columns 8-11 stress the new god's ineffable quality and suggest Akhenaten's special relationship with the deity—which Akhenaten would reiterate again and again in references to the Sun-disc as "his father" and to himself as the "fair child of the Sun-disc." The intimacy of this relationship is often graphically illustrated: The rays of light from the Sun-disc end in human-like hands that fondle and protect the beloved son, Akhenaten, and his wife, Nefertity.

Given the extremely fragmentary nature of the text, however, several problems remain. We would love to know what exactly is implied by the verb *3bw* (translated above as "ceased") when it is applied to the gods and their statuary. Does it mean, for instance, that the Sun-disc has thrown over all the other gods in the Egyptian pantheon? Or does it mean that these gods were the creation of the Sun-disc in the first place? Or is Akhenaten suggesting that the other gods never really existed at all? Another question: Is it only coincidental that the most frequent sobriquet of Amenophis III, Akhenaten's father, was "the Dazzling Sun-disc"? Perhaps there is more here than meets the eye—that is, maybe Akhenaten conflates the Sun-disc and his dead father in a way that we don't yet understand. Also, we would like to know if the text represents a private prayer or a public message to Akhenaten's court, in which the pharaoh instructs his subjects about the nature and power of the new god. Members of the king's

The Cult of the Sun-disc.
Akhenaten makes an
offering to his sole, univer-
sal god, Aten, symbolized
by the Sun-disc, in this
detail from a relief found
in Amarna. (The com-
plete relief, which includes
a depiction of Akhenaten's
wife Nefertity making an
identical offering, is
shown on a color plate on
page 97.) The rays from
the Sun-disc, showering
the pharaoh, end in
human hands, which may
be presenting an ankh
(the symbol of life) to the
royal figure.

ERICH LESSING

Amarna coterie constantly tell us in their biographies how wonderful the king's "teaching" was and how they all adhered to it. Is the present inscription an example of such teaching?

Akhenaten's exaltation of the Sun-disc as supreme, self-begotten and all-powerful leads us to expect to find intolerance toward elements that did not fit into his thinking. And we do. His attempted destruction of Amun—by defacing the god's name and image—is well known. Less well known is the fact that Akhenaten banished Amun's high-priest to work in the quarries. While there is no evidence that Akhenaten moved actively to close the temples of Amun, he did divert the income from these temples to his new Sun-disc shrines. His boyhood tutor, butler and master of alimentation, Parennefer, threatened those who refused to comport with the new program. An inscription on Parennefer's Theban tomb reads: "Now the Sun knows which is the servant that is diligent with respect to offerings. The servant who is not diligent with respect to the offerings of the Sun-disc gives himself over into thy [the king's] power; for the grain imposts of every other god are measured merely in small amounts, but for the Sun-disc they are measured in superabundance."

Akhenaten was clearly a monotheist. All the well-known ingredients are present: the revelation-cum-teaching, the belligerent iconoclasm, the denial of the plurality of the Supernatural, the anathematization of other "gods," the purging of forms of religious expression. He believed in a single, universal god, Aten, who had created the world and who continued to affect the world through His active presence. But Akhenaten's religion did not go much further; he promulgated his belief in the supreme Sun-disc by having temples built and hymns composed—and by disfiguring the "false" gods—and that was largely that.

Before much of the archaeological evidence from Thebes and from Tell el-Amarna became available, wishful thinking sometimes turned Akhenaten into a humane teacher of the true God, a mentor of Moses, a Christlike figure, a philosopher before his time. But these imaginary creatures are now fading away one by one as the historical reality gradually emerges. There is little or no evidence to support the notion that Akhenaten was a progenitor of the full-blown monotheism that we find in the Bible. The monotheism of the Hebrew Bible and the New Testament had its own separate development—one that began more than half a millenium after the pharoah's death.

FOLK RELIGION IN EARLY ISRAEL: DID YAHWEH HAVE A CONSORT?

William G. Dever

Does the Hebrew Bible provide an adequate account of the religious beliefs and practices of ancient Israel? The answer is a resounding no. The Bible deals extensively with religion and even seems preoccupied with the subject; and it does provide a record of a developing monotheism associated with the reforms of the Judahite kings Hezekiah (727-698 B.C.E.) and Josiah (639-608 B.C.E.). But it is ultimately limited as a source of information about the great variety of Israelite cult practices.

The Hebrew Bible is not an eyewitness account. Rather, it was edited into its present form during the post-Exilic period (beginning in the latter part of the sixth century B.C.E.), centuries after the events it purports to record. It thus reflects the religious crisis of the Diaspora community of that time. The Bible is also limited by the fact that its final editors—the primary shapers of the tradition—belonged to orthodox nationalist Yahwist parties (the Priestly and Deuteronomic schools)* that were hardly representative of the majority in ancient Israel. The Bible, as a theologian friend reminds me, is "a minority report." Largely written by priests, prophets and scribes who were intellectuals and religious reformers, the Bible is highly idealistic. It presents us not so much with a picture of what Israelite religion really was but of what it should have been.

The Bible is an elitist document in another sense as well: It was written and edited exclusively by men. It therefore represents their concerns—those of the Establishment of the time—to the virtual exclusion of all else. In particular, the Bible's focus is on political history, the deeds of great men, public events, affairs of state, and great ideas and institutions. It almost totally ignores private and family religion and women's cults; "folk religion," the cultic practice of the majority in ancient Israel and Judah, is passed over almost without a word.[1]

If the biblical texts alone are an inadequate witness to ancient Israelite religion, where else can we turn for information?

Modern archaeology has brought to light a mass of new, factual, tangible information about the history and religion of ancient Israel. This material is incredibly varied, almost unlimited in quantity, and has the advantage of being more objective than texts—that is, less deliberately edited. Archaeology also possesses a unique potential for illuminating folk religion, in contrast to the official religion of the texts, because material remains, unlike the texts, do not favor elites; and material remains present evidence of concrete religious practices rather than abstract theological formulations.

---

*According to the documentary hypothesis, the Pentateuch was composed at different stages in Israel's history by four different writers or schools, indicated by the letters J (the Yahwist or, in German, Jahwist source), E (the Elohist source), P (the Priestly code) and D (the Deuteronomic source). The Deuteronomic source is also generally credited with the books of Joshua, Judges, Samuel and Kings.

Archaeology does not simply tell us what priests and clerics think the people *should have done*; it provides an account of what they *actually did*.[2] The abundance of recent archaeological data forces us to rewrite all previous histories of ancient Israelite religion and, in particular, to address the issue of whether Israel was truly monotheistic during the monarchical period.

Cultic Sites in Ancient Israel

Several recently excavated sites in Israel have produced materials that are clearly cultic in nature, some of them no doubt what the Bible is referring to when it condemns *bamot*, or "high places" (for example, 2 Kings 23:8). We shall move from north to south and from the period of the Judges to the monarchy, that is, from Iron Age I (1200-1000 B.C.E.) through Iron Age II (1000-586 B.C.E.).

The Bull Site. A small open-air hilltop sanctuary in the tribal territory of Manasseh, dating to the 12th century B.C.E., was excavated in 1981 by Amihai Mazar. It features a central paved area with a large standing stone (a biblical *massebah*) and an altar-like installation, the whole enclosed by a wall. The only material recovered consists of a few early Iron Age I sherds, some fragments of metal and of a terra-cotta offering stand, and a splendidly preserved bronze zebu bull (see color plate, p. 98). The bull, possibly a votive statue, is almost identical to a bronze bull found by Yigael Yadin at Hazor in a Late Bronze Age (1550-1200 B.C.E.) context. The principal epithet of El, the chief male deity of the Canaanite pantheon in pre-Israelite times, was "Bull." Thus the Manasseh shrine or sanctuary—the only clear Israelite cultic installation yet found from the period of the Judges—was probably associated not with Yahweh but with the old Canaanite deity El.[3]

Dan. The distinctive mound of Tel Dan, one of the early capitals of the northern kingdom of Israel, has been excavated since

1966 by Avraham Biran. At the highest point on the northern end of the mound is an impressive installation from the tenth to ninth centuries B.C.E. It consists of a large podium, or altar, approached by a flight of steps, all in fine ashlar (chisel-dressed) masonry, and an adjoining three-room structure, probably an example of the biblical *lishkāh*, or sanctuary. In one room of the sanctuary, archaeologists found a low stone altar, an ash pit and three iron shovels. This installation is probably best understood as an example of the enigmatic Canaanite-style high place (*bamah*) that is condemned in the Hebrew Bible. It may even be the very "house [or temple] on a high place" mentioned in 1 Kings 12:31.

Other materials found within the precinct include an olive oil press, used for liturgical purposes; large and small four-horned altars, which are alluded to in several biblical passages; a bronze-working installation; a fine priestly scepter; seven-spouted lamps; a *naos* (a household temple model or shrine); several dice; and male and female figurines. This cult installation lasted into the seventh century B.C.E., dramatically illustrating that "non-Establishment" cults did exist in the early monarchy as well as throughout Israel's and Judah's history.[4] When mentioned at all, these cults were condemned by the southern Israelite writers and editors of the Bible, who were loyal to the Temple in Jerusalem.

Tell el-Farʿah (North). Referred to as Tirzah in the Bible, Tell el-Farʿah (North) served as the temporary capital of the northern kingdom of Israel in the early ninth century B.C.E. The site was excavated by Père Roland de Vaux from 1946 to 1960. Just inside the city gate is a *massebah* and an olive press—no doubt part of the "gate-shrine" referred to in the Bible. De Vaux also found numerous tenth- and ninth-century B.C.E. female figurines (some of the earliest known Asherah figurines) and a terracotta *naos*. This *naos*, to judge from other contemporaneous examples, would have had a deity, or a pair of deities, standing in the doorway; one of them would have been Asherah, the

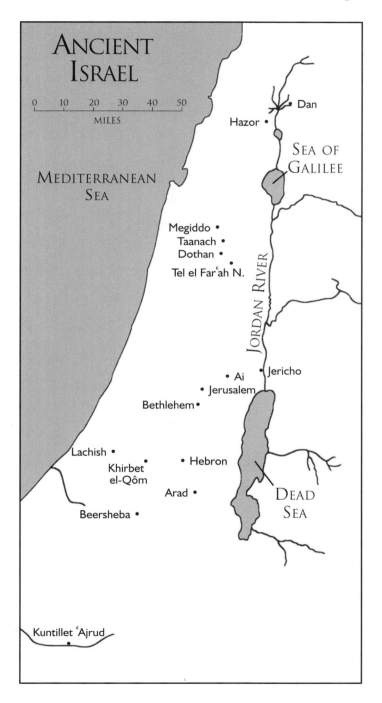

ANCIENT
ISRAEL

0   10   20   30   40   50
MILES

MEDITERRANEAN
SEA

Dan

Hazor •

SEA OF
GALILEE

Megiddo •
Taanach •
Dothan •
Tel el Farʿah N.

JORDAN RIVER

• Ai   • Jericho
• Jerusalem
Bethlehem •

Lachish •
        •
Khirbet
el-Qôm

• Hebron

Arad •

Beersheba •

DEAD
SEA

Kuntillet ʿAjrud

TEL DAN EXCAVATIONS, HEBREW UNION COLLEGE/A. BIRAN

A broad staircase (lower left) at Tel Dan leads to a raised platform of limestone blocks—probably an example of a "high place" (bamah) *condemned in the Bible. Excavator Avraham Biran dates this shrine to the reign of the first ruler of the northern kingdom of Israel, Jereboam I (928-907 B.C.E.), who is said to have constructed shrines at Bethel and Dan to compete with the Jerusalem Temple (1 Kings 12:30-31). Adjacent to the shrine, Biran uncovered a 60-foot-long rectangular structure (see photo and plan opposite), called a* lishkah

ZEV RADOVAN

ZEV RADOVAN

(chamber), built in the ninth or eighth century B.C.E. apparently to accommodate priestly functions. In one room of the lishkah *(top of photo) rested a three-foot-square stone structure (opposite, top left), which Biran interprets as an altar. A bowl buried in the hole next to the altar contained ashes, probably from incense offerings, and nearby lay three iron incense shovels (opposite, bottom). All of these finds at the Dan shrine suggest the cultic character of the site.*

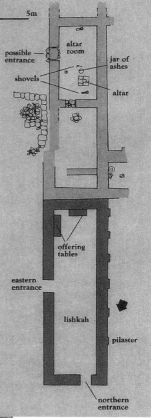

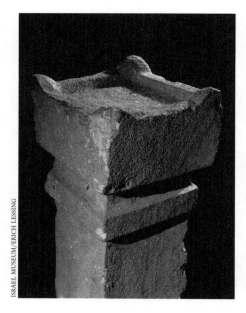

ISRAEL MUSEUM/ERICH LESSING

Megiddo horned altar.
Measuring 21 inches high, this
limestone altar with horn-shaped
projections at the corners was
discovered at Megiddo in a
tenth- or ninth-century B.C.E.
context. Numerous small altars
dating from the tenth to seventh
centuries B.C.E. have been
uncovered at various sites in
Israel—suggesting that the mak-
ing of offerings of grain, oil,
wine or incense to Yahweh or
other deities was a widespread
cultic practice.

Canaanite mother goddess. Tell el-Farʿah (North)'s Canaanite temple model/shrine was in use during the very period of the Solomonic Temple in Jerusalem, where, at least according to the biblical writers, all worship was centralized.[5]

Megiddo. Another example of supposedly prohibited local object of worship is a household shrine found in tenth-century B.C.E. strata at Megiddo (see color plate, p. 98), a Solomonic regional capital in the north. The shrine consists of several cult vessels and small four-horned limestone altars, of a type found at many Israelite sites. The altars were probably used for incense offerings, which were integral to the official worship described in the biblical texts (though the Bible does not refer specifically to small horned altars, only to much larger examples, as in 1 Kings 1:50-51).[6]

Taanach. A few miles southeast of Megiddo lies its sister city, Taanach, where even more substantial tenth-century B.C.E. cultic remains have come to light. A shrine there contains a large olive press, a mold for making terra-cotta female figurines like those from Tell el-Farʿah (North), and a hoard of astragali, or knuckle-bones, used in divination rites.

More remarkable are two large multitiered terra-cotta offering stands. One, found long ago by a German excavation, depicts ranks of lions. The other, from the American excavations of Paul Lapp, has four tiers and is probably best understood as a temple model (see color plate, p. 100). The top tier, or story, shows a quadruped carrying a winged Sun-disc on its back. The next row down depicts the doorway of the temple, which stands empty, perhaps to signify that the deity of this house (in Hebrew, *beit* [house] means "tem-ple" when used in connection with a deity) is invisible. The third row down has a pair of sphinxes, or winged lions, one on each side, which probably represent the biblical cherubim depicted in the Solomonic Temple (see 1 Kings 8:6-7).

The bottom row of this Taanach stand is startling: It has two similar flanking lions, with a smiling nude female figure standing between them, holding them by the ears. Who is this enigmatic figure? She can be no other than Asherah, the Canaanite mother goddess. Asherah is known throughout the Levant in this period as the "Lion Lady,"[7] and she is often depicted nude, riding on the back of a lion. One side of a 12th- or 11th-century B.C.E. inscribed arrowhead from the Jerusalem area reads, "servant of the Lion Lady"; the arrowhead probably belonged to a professional archer, who thus named his patroness.[8] On the other side of the arrowhead appears the archer's name, Ben-Anat, or "son of Anat"; Anat is another name for the old Canaanite mother goddess. We can only wonder what a model temple possibly depicting an invisible Yahweh and a very visible Asherah was doing at Israelite Taanach in the days of Solomon and the Jerusalem Temple. This is a remarkable piece of ancient Israelite iconography. As we shall see, however, there is an abundance of evidence for the cult of Asherah in Israel during the biblical period.[8]

Jerusalem. Of the many pieces of archaeological evidence of religion from Jerusalem, only a few can be singled out here. A rock-cut tomb on the grounds of the Dominican École Biblique et Archéologique Française, long known but only recently dated to the eighth to seventh centuries B.C.E., has benches for the corpses that feature headrests carved in the shape of the Hathor wig. This distinctive bouffant wig was worn in Egypt by Qudshu, the Egyptian cow goddess, who was identified with the popular Canaanite goddess Asherah. Thus, even in Jerusalem, the spiritual center of biblical religion, a Judahite woman could be buried with her head resting in a wig that was strongly associated with the Canaanite goddess Asherah.[9]

Another tomb from the late seventh century B.C.E., found near St. Andrew's Church of Scotland, contained similar benches

The southern limit of ancient Israel, Beersheba (above) was excavated by
Yohanan Aharoni in the early 1970s. Among his finds were well-dressed stones
built into the walls under a rampart dating to the late eighth century B.C.E.
When assembled, these stones formed a cubical altar about 5 feet high by 5 feet
wide by 5 feet long (opposite); recent evidence suggests, however, that the altar
was actually 9 feet long. Contrary to biblical law (Exodus 20:25), the altar
was made of hewn stones and had a serpent incised on one of its blocks. Its
top stones were blackened, suggesting that burnt sacrifices (probably animal
sacrifices) were offered on this large altar. Aharoni concluded that the
Beersheba altar had been deliberatly destroyed during the religious reform
of the Judahite king Hezekiah (727-698 B.C.E.)—who sought to restrict all
cultic practices to the worship of Yahweh in Jerusalem.

with headrests, as well as two tiny silver scrolls (see color plate, p. 99).
Both scrolls are inscribed with passages found in the priestly blessing
of Numbers 6:24-26. These scrolls date to about 600 B.C.E., making them by far our oldest surviving source of a biblical text—at least
four centuries older than any of the Dead Sea Scrolls. This bit of
Scripture, however, was used not for edification but for "magic,"
which was strictly forbidden in orthodox Israelite religion. What we

TEL AVIV UNIVERSITY

The Holy of Holies (*opposite, top*), *or innermost room, of the temple to Yahweh at Arad was entered through a small niche flanked by two limestone incense altars; at the rear of the chamber stood two* masseboth, *or sacred standing stones (the altars and* masseboth *shown here are replicas, the orginals having been removed to the Israel Museum in Jerusalem). In front of the Holy of Holies but within the temple compound stood a large altar (opposite, bottom), about 4.5 feet high and 7.5 feet long and wide, probably used for animal sacrifices; cut into the altar's platform were channels for draining off blood and fat. Found near the altar were a small bronze lion (above), often associated with the Canaanite goddess Asherah, and a red-slip pottery stand (right), probably used for incense offerings. Built in the tenth century B.C.E., the Arad temple remained in use until it was destroyed during the religious reforms of either Hezekiah in the late eighth century B.C.E. or Josiah in the late seventh.*

TEL AVIV UNIVERSITY

have here is a biblical text that was engraved on silver, rolled up, put on a string and worn around the neck as an amulet—a good-luck charm.[10] And there are many more archaeological examples of such magical or superstitious practices, from both Israel and Judah, some of them invoking foreign deities, such as the Egyptian gods Bes and Osiris. Bible scholars have paid little attention to archaeological finds of this sort, but they should: Such objects illustrate the prevalence of the folk religion so vigorously condemned in the Bible as idol worship, or the use of *mipleset*, "an abominable thing" (1 Kings 15:13//2 Chronicles 15:16).

Beersheba. Marking the southern limits of the settled zone in monarchical times (as in the biblical phrase "from Dan to Beersheba"), Beersheba was excavated by Yohanan Aharoni from 1969 to 1975. Among the most spectacular finds were several large dressed blocks of stone that make up a monumental four-horned altar. Over five feet tall, this is one of only two examples of such large altars that archaeologists have brought to light (the other is at Dan). Its stones, however, were not recovered *in situ* but were found in secondary use, built into the walls of later storehouses near the city gate.

Where did the Beersheba altar originally stand, and why was it dismantled? Aharoni argued that his "basement building"—a large structure set into an unusually deep foundation trench that obliterated lower levels—was the site of what had once been a large temple, where the altar had originally stood. If so, the temple may have been destroyed during the eighth-century B.C.E. religious reforms of Hezekiah, who pulled down the high places and their altars (2 Chronicles 29-32). As though to confirm Aharoni's theory, a large krater (a two-handled pot) found nearby is inscribed in Hebrew, *qōdesh*, which means "sacred" or "set apart" (for cultic use).

The Beersheba finds are the first actual archaeological evidence confirming the religious reforms of Judahite kings. They also provide evidence of the *need* for such reforms: The religious activities denounced by the biblical prophets as the worship of "foreign gods" were evidently widespread.[11]

Arad. Not far to the east of Beersheba is Arad, a small Judahite hilltop fortress and sanctuary also excavated by Aharoni. The dating and interpretation of the various tenth- to sixth-century B.C.E. phases remain controversial because of faulty excavation methods and the lack of final reports. Yet for our purposes, the main points are clear. One corner of the ninth- to eighth-century B.C.E. walled citadel is occupied by a three-room temple, very similar in plan to the partly contemporaneous Temple in Jerusalem. The outer area (the biblical *ʿulām*, vestibule) is actually an open-air courtyard with a large stone altar, at the base of which were found burned animal bones, a terra-cotta offering stand, a fine crouching bronze lion and two shallow platters inscribed with the Hebrew letters *qop kap*, probably an abbreviation for *qōdesh hā-kōhanîm*, meaning "sacred" or "set apart for the priests." And several priestly families with names identical to priestly families mentioned in the Bible are listed on ostraca (inscribed potsherds) found at Arad—one of which (number 18) also mentions the "house [temple] of Yahweh."

The temple's main central chamber (the biblical *heikhal*) is a smaller room with low benches, undoubtedly for the presentation of offerings. The inner chamber (the biblical *dvir*, Holy of Holies) is a still smaller niche. The steps to this inner chamber hold two stylized horned altars containing an oily organic substance that suggests incense. Against the chamber's back wall rest two sacred standing stones (*masseboth*) with traces of red paint, one of them smaller than the other.

Since these altars and standing stones had been carefully laid down and floored over in a later stage of this building, Aharoni argued that the Arad temple presents additional archaeological evidence of the reforms of Hezekiah (or, according to other scholars, Josiah), who abolished local sanctuaries in favor of the

Jerusalem Temple. I would go further: Both the bronze lion and the pair of standing stones show that Asherah, the Lion Lady, was worshiped *alongside* Yahweh at Arad, perhaps for a century or more, until this became a problem for religious reformers. Is this the sort of syncretism that the prophets decried? Or was Asherah so thoroughly assimilated into the Israelite cult from early times that most Israelites considered her to be native to their beliefs and practices—that is, associated with Yahweh, and perhaps even his consort?[12]

Kuntillet ʿAjrud. As though to answer this question, dramatic textual evidence of Asherah has recently come to light at two sites. Kuntillet ʿAjrud is a hilltop caravanserai, or stopover station, in the remote eastern Sinai desert. It was discovered by the British explorer Edward Palmer in 1878 and excavated in 1978 by the Israeli archaeologist Ze'ev Meshel. Again, the finds are controversial

Kuntillet ʿAjrud *(opposite), in Sinai, has supplied some of the earliest Hebrew fragments with religious text. The fragment at right (shown also in the drawing), from an eighth-century B.C.E.* pithos *(storage jar), contains the blessing "By Yahweh of Samaria and His Asherah."*

In the crude drawing below the inscription, the bovine-like figure may be the "Young Bull of Samaria" (see Hosea 8:6)—the idolatrous form of Yahweh wor-shiped in the northern kingdom of Israel—while the female figure by his side may be Asherah, who in the Canaanite pantheon was the consort of the chief god El, often pictured as a bull. (According to some scholars, however, the fore-ground figures are depictions of the Egyptian god Bes, and the lyre player is just a musician.) Also on this pithos *is a drawing of a tree flanked by ibexes (see p. 78)—which may be another depiction of the semidivine asherah figure.*

and published only in preliminary reports. Yet the impact of the material known so far is revolutionary for our understanding of ancient Israelite religion. The main structure at Kuntillet ʿAjrud, from the eighth century B.C.E., is a large rectangular fort with double walls, corner towers and a central open courtyard—similar to other known Iron Age fortresses in the Negev. The entrance area, however, is unique. It is approached through a white plaster esplanade, which leads into a passageway flanked by two plastered side rooms with low benches, behind which are cupboard-like chambers. These chambers are clearly *favissae*, storage areas for discarded votives and cult offerings, many examples of which have been found at Bronze Age and Iron Age sanctuaries. The benches are obviously not seats but platforms for offerings, a type of installation that also has many parallels.

Any doubt about the existence of a shrine here in the ʿAjrud gateway (and surprisingly enough, some scholars do doubt it) is removed by even a cursory examination of the finds. These include a large stone votive bowl inscribed in Hebrew: "(Belonging) to Obadaiah son of Adnah; may he be blessed by Yahweh." On several large storage jars are painted motifs and scenes: a processional of strangely garbed individuals; the familiar "tree of life," with flanking ibexes (see drawing on p. 78); lions; and striking representations of the Egyptian good-luck god Bes and a seated half-nude female figure playing a lyre, whose distinctive lion-throne suggests that she is a goddess (as we also find gods and goddesses seated on lion-thrones elsewhere in the ancient Near East). A Hebrew inscription on one storage jar is a blessing formula, ending with the words "by Yahweh of Samaria and his Asherah."

Some biblical scholars understand the Hebrew word *ăšērâ* (plural *ăšērîm*), which occurs some 40 times in the Hebrew Bible, as referring only to a wooden image of some kind—a pole or tree—commonly associated with the goddess Asherah. Yet a growing number of scholars are beginning to recognize the true significance of these images: Whether "a/Asherah" at ʿAjrud refers to the goddess herself or merely her symbol—an "agent of blessing" that could be invoked alongside Yahweh—there was a widespread perception in ancient Israel of the goddess's *reality*, which gave the symbolism its efficacy. In either case, despite the abhorrence of some prophets and priests, the old Canaanite Asherah was alive and well in many circles in Israel—at least through the eighth and seventh centuries B.C.E., when attempts to discredit her began.

The archaeological evidence from the Kuntillet ʿAjrud texts alone should force us to rethink much of what scholars have written about "normative" religion, about monotheism, in ancient Israel. The ideal religion formulated late in the Hebrew Bible is one thing; actual religious practices are another, reflecting a popular religion that we would scarcely have known about if not for the accidents of archaeological preservation and discovery.[13]

Khirbet el-Qôm. The ʿAjrud texts help corroborate the meaning of an eighth-century B.C.E. Judahite tomb inscription near Hebron, which I discovered in 1968. Although parts of the reading are difficult and controversial, the best interpretation goes something like this:

> ʾUriyahu the Prince; this is his inscription.
> May ʾUriyahu be blessed by Yahweh,
> For from his enemies he has saved him by his
>   Asherah.

Virtually all scholars now agree that the reading "by his a/Asherah" in line 3 is certain; the phrase is identical to that at ʿAjrud and presents the same problems of interpretation. Nevertheless, considering that we have only a handful of ancient Hebrew inscriptions from tombs or cultic contexts, the fact that two of them mention "a/Asherah" in the context of a blessing is striking. It would appear that in nonbiblical texts such an expression was common,

God's hand? *An enigmatic symbol accompanies an inscription that solicits the blessing of Yahweh and "his Asherah," on this relief carving from an eighth-century B.C.E. tomb in Khirbet el-Qôm, near Hebron. References to Asherah here and at Kuntillet 'Ajrud suggest that some Israelites believed that Yahweh had a divine consort—which helps explain why Asherah (whether conceived as a kind of divine being or as the sacred tree of life) is so scathingly criticized in the Bible.*

an acceptable expression of Israelite Yahwism throughout much of the monarchy. Thus Asherah was commonly thought of as the consort of Yahweh, or perhaps as a hypostasis of Yahweh—that is, a personification of some aspect of Yahweh (his wisdom or presence, for example). The orthodox textual tradition has, in effect, purged the Bible of many original references to the goddess

Asherah, as well as downplayed the remaining references to the point that many are scarcely intelligible.[14]

Artifacts of the Israelite Cult

In addition to the cultic sites, we now have many individual artifacts that reflect the variety of religious beliefs and practices in ancient Israel and Judah.

Offering stands. Dozens of Israelite terra-cotta offering stands date from the 12th to the 7th century B.C.E. They continue a long Bronze Age tradition of cult stands throughout the ancient Near East, which, as we know from seal impressions and paintings, were used to present gifts of food, drink and perhaps incense to the gods. Such rituals became part of the standard cult in ancient Israel, as we know from many biblical texts, so there must have been at one time a fairly elaborate paraphernalia.[15] It is therefore curious that the Hebrew Bible never even hints at the use of offering stands. Is it possible that the biblical writers were unaware of such widespread practices? Or did they simply believe that the sharpest sign of disapproval would be to disdain mentioning them?

Some of the Israelite offering stands are rather plain, with no obvious symbolic significance. But others, like the elaborate tenth-century B.C.E. Taanach stand (see color plate, p. 100), are full of Canaanite religious imagery. One of the most enigmatic is a 12th-century B.C.E. stand from Ai, an Israelite site from the period of the Judges. This stand has numerous fenestrations, or "windows," probably to facilitate incense burning; it also features a curious row of well-modeled, human feet, which protrude from the bottom. A foot-fetish cult?[16] In any case, the omission of any reference whatsoever in the Hebrew Bible to these common offering stands, when the texts are so preoccupied with sacrificial rituals, should give us pause. What *are* the biblical writers and editors describing: actual religious practices in ancient Israel or their own idealized, theologized reconstruction of what should have taken place?

Altars. Some four-horned limestone altars, like the one from Beersheba, are very large. But most—and at least 40 are now known—are miniature, from about 1 foot to 3 feet high. These small horned altars, dating from the tenth to the sixth century B.C.E., are found all over Israel and Judah in cultic, domestic and even industrial contexts.

Although the significance of the horn-like projections at the four corners is uncertain, they may be connected with older Bronze Age bull cults well known throughout the eastern Mediterranean

Ai offering stand.
Throughout the Iron Age, ceramic stands were used to make offerings of incense, oil or food to the deity. The Ai stand, found in an Israelite site from the period of the Judges (12th century B.C.E.), contains numerous fenestrations (windows), perhaps to allow worshipers to place burning incense inside the stand and to allow the smoke to escape. Offering stands are so common in the biblical period that it is puzzling that they are not mentioned at all in the Bible.

world. As we have noted, the title "Bull" was used for the deity El in the Canaanite pantheon. It is also significant that when the biblical writers want to describe the Israelites' apostasy, they tell stories of the people setting up a bronze calf at Mt. Sinai or of Jeroboam erecting a golden calf in his newly established royal sanctuary at Dan (1 Kings 12:28,29) after the death of Solomon and the secession of the northern tribes.

But once again the biblical writers and editors are completely silent: The texts contain no hint of these small horned altars, even though they were probably used for burning incense, a practice described in detail in the Bible. So what is going on? When the Bible describes local altars being torn down in religious reforms, it surely is not referring to these small, portable monoliths. But in that case, what is being referred to and why do the texts fail to give us any details? If they did, we might be better equipped to identify monumental altars, of which we have no certain examples, as well as the miniature varieties. As it is, the facts on the ground do not coincide with the biblical descriptions, indicating at the very least two differing perceptions, if not religious realities: that of the Bible's writers and editors, and that of everyone else.[17]

Cult vessels. Numerous exotic terra-cotta vessels and implements, many of them unparalleled, are best understood as cultic in nature. They were no doubt used for ritual purposes, even though the exact manner in which they were employed, as well as the rationale behind them, may elude us.

One class of such cultic vessels is the *naos*, or temple model, of which we have several Israelite examples. The *naos* continues a long Bronze Age tradition of household models and shrines, often with depictions of a deity or pair of deities standing in the doorway. The frequent representation of lions, doves and Hathor wigs suggests that these model shrines were used in the veneration of Asherah, perhaps by women at local shrines or in domestic cults.[18]

Another class of cult vessel is the *kernos*, or "trick-vessel," closely connected with Cyprus and perhaps introduced into Israel by the Sea Peoples or the Phoenicians. These are usually small bowls with a hollow rim that conducts fluid; the rim communicates with hollow animal heads attached to the bottom of the rim. When filled with a liquid, such as olive oil or wine, these bowls can be tilted to make the heads pour or appear to drink. While some scholars dismiss *kernoi* as simply toys, it is more reasonable to presume that these complex, exotic vessels were used in the cult for libation offerings. Such offerings are frequently mentioned in biblical texts; but again there is no mention of *kernoi* or of any other libation vessels that we can identify archaeologically.[19]

Also common are terra-cotta zoomorphic figurines, especially from eighth- and seventh-century B.C.E. Judahite tombs. Most are quadrupeds, like horses (sometimes with riders), cows or bulls, but other farm animals are also portrayed (one depicts a three-legged chicken). Some of these animal figurines are hollow and may have served as libation vessels. Others are more enigmatic. The horse-and-rider figurines and the quadrupeds with Sun-discs on their heads have been connected with biblical references to Josiah cleansing the Jerusalem Temple of the "horses ... dedicated to the sun" and "chariots of the sun" (see 2 Kings 23:11). This is an obvious allusion to Assyrian and Babylonian solar and astral cults, which probably made serious inroads into Israelite and Judahite religion in the eighth to sixth centuries B.C.E. and which met with strong prophetic condemnation.[20]

Archaeology has recovered many other terra-cotta items that almost certainly had a cultic function. Particularly common in tombs are miniature models of household furniture, such as chairs, couches and beds. They undoubtedly were meant to accompany the dead into the afterlife and thus must have had some religious (or magical) significance. The same is probably true of small stone-filled rattles. Like the *kernoi*, these rattles are sometimes interpreted merely as toys, but this view simply highlights our ignorance (or lack

Terra-cotta figurines, just a few inches tall, are especially common in Iron Age Judah, where they are often found within the remains of houses. The pillar figurines depicting women with prominent breasts probably represent one of the Canaanite goddesses, Asherah or Astarte, and were likely associated with rituals involving fertility or a safe pregnancy. The clay ram at right, about 4 inches long, probably also dates to the Iron Age.

of imagination) in dealing with the ancient cult. On the other hand, some clay vessels, such as perforated tripod censors, obviously had a cultic function, and we must try to understand what that was.

Figurines. By far the most intriguing cultic artifacts that archaeologists have recovered are more than 2,000 mold-made terra cotta female figurines, found in all sorts of contexts. They depict a nude female frontally; in the earlier examples, the figure often clutches a tambourine (or mold for bread) or occasionally an infant, whereas the later Judahite examples emphasize the figure's prominent breasts. In contrast to the typical Late Bronze Age plaques depicting the mother goddess with large hips and an exaggerated pubic triangle, the Israelite figurines usually render the lower body simply as a pillar (thus the name "pillar figurines"); the pillar may represent a tree, a motif often connected with Asherah. These comparatively chaste portrayals may indicate that Asherah/Anat—the consort of the male deity in Canaan, with her more blatantly sexual characteristics—has now been supplanted by a concept of the female deity as principally a mother and a patroness of mothers. William F. Albright's designation of these as "*dea nutrix* figurines" (nurturing goddesses) may be close to the mark. More recently, Ziony Zevit has aptly termed the female figurines "prayers in clay"—in this case, invocations to the mother goddess Asherah.[21]

It is surprising that so many biblical scholars and archaeologists are reluctant to conclude *anything* about these female figurines. Some claim they are merely toys—what I call the "Barbie doll syndrome." Others say we simply do not and cannot know what they are. But their cultic connections are obvious. In ancient Israel most women, having been excluded from public life and the conduct of official political and religious functions, necessarily occupied themselves with domestic concerns. Predominant among these was reproduction—conception, childbirth and lactation. But there were also other extremely important concerns connected with rites of passage, marriages and funerals, and the maintenance and survival of the family. To be sure, men were involved in some of these domestic activities, but "the religion of hearth and home" fell mainly to women in Israel, as it did everywhere in the ancient world. It would not be surprising if Yahweh—portrayed almost exclusively as a male deity, preoccupied with the political history of the nation—seemed remote and unconcerned with women's needs or even hostile to them. Thus half the population of ancient Israel, women, may have felt closer to a female deity and identified more easily with her. That deity would have been the old Canaanite mother goddess, who was still widely venerated in many guises in the Levantine Iron Age, and indeed much later.[22]

Toward a Definition of Popular Religion

With all this new archaeological evidence, we are prompted to ask: If the Bible records the religious practices only of elites, what did everyone else do? What *is* "popular religion?"[23]

One source of information is those texts of the Hebrew Bible that *condemn* certain religious practices. This involves a reasonable assumption, namely that the biblical prophets, priests and reformers knew what they were talking about—that the religious situation they complained about was real, not invented by them as a foil for their revisionist message. Ironically, in denouncing popular religious practices, the biblical writers unwittingly preserved chance descriptions of those practices. (That is not to say, however, that the same writers and editors in their zeal for orthodoxy did not deliberately suppress much information about popular religion that we should like to have.) Fortunately, archaeology has supplied much supplementary information; it has given us valuable clues on how to read between the lines of biblical texts.[24]

Consider two examples of how we might read the textual and the archaeological records together. Jeremiah 7:18 offers a telling description of what must have been a common family ritual, although one decried by the prophet: "The children gather wood, the fathers kindle fire, and the women knead dough to make cakes for the Queen of Heaven." The latter is either Asherah or her counterpart Astarte (often coalesced, along with Anat, into a single figure in the Iron Age), of whom archaeology has supplied many,

many images. An even fuller account of what was really going on in Judahite times is provided by the lengthy description in 2 Kings 23 of King Josiah's reforms in the late seventh century B.C.E. Most biblical scholars have interpreted this passage as a piece of Deuteronomic propaganda, not as an accurate historical account of the king's activities. But whether or not Josiah's reform succeeded, the description of practices posing the *need* for such reform may have been based on the actual religious situation. It appears that it was; indeed, every single religious object or practice proscribed in 2 Kings 23 (for example, images of Asherah and offerings made on high places) can readily be illustrated by archaeological discoveries. The terminology of the text is not at all enigmatic; it is a clear reflection of the religious reality in monarchical times.[25]

Archaeology, supplemented by the biblical text, provides a highly accurate picture of popular religion. (1) It is noninstitutional, lying outside priestly control or state sponsorship. (2) Because it is nonauthoritarian, popular religion is inclusive rather than exclusive; it appeals especially to minorities and to the disenfranchised (almost all women in ancient Israel); in both belief and practice it tends to be eclectic and syncretistic. (3) Popular religion focuses more on individual piety and domestic or communal rhythms of life than on elaborate public ritual, more on cult than on intellectual formulations such as theology. (4) By definition, popular religion is less literate (though not any less complex or sophisticated) and thus may be inclined to leave behind more archaeological traces than literary records, more ostraca and graffiti than classical texts, more cultic paraphernalia than Scripture. (5) Despite these apparent dichotomies, popular religion overlaps significantly with official religion, if only by sheer force of numbers of practitioners; it often sees itself as equally legitimate, and it attempts to secure the same benefits as all religion does—the individual's sense of integration with nature and society, health and prosperity, and ultimate well-being.

The major elements of popular religion in ancient Israel probably included the following: frequenting *bamot* and other local shrines; making images; venerating *ăšērîm*, whether as sacred trees or as images of the goddess; performing rituals having to do with childbirth and child-care; participating in pilgrimages and saints' festivals; celebrating planting and harvest festivals; holding *mārzēāḥ* feasts (Canaanite festivals of mourning); conducting funerary rites, such as libations for the dead; baking cakes for the "Queen of Heaven" (probably Astarte); wailing over Tammuz (the old Mesopotamian consort of the female deity Ishtar); worshiping solar and astral deities; practicing divination and sorcery; and perhaps sacrificing children. These and other elements of folk religion are often assumed to have characterized the religion of "hearth and home" and thus to have been almost exclusively the province of women. That assumption carries with it a note of condescension. After all, women in ancient Israel were largely illiterate and marginalized; they played an insignificant role in the sociopolitical processes that shaped Israelite life and institutions. Nevertheless, family religion in ancient Israel must have involved men as well, especially in rural areas far from the influence of the elite circles of Jerusalem. Asherah, who brought life, may well have been the patroness of men as well as of women.

Why has the role of popular religion and the cult of the mother goddess in ancient Israel been neglected, misunderstood or downplayed by the majority of Bible scholars? One reason is that most Bible students share the elitist biases of the biblical writers themselves. Another reason is that the last 200 years of biblical scholarship have been largely shaped by Protestant scholars, who have preferred theology over cult (that is, over religious *practices* of any kind). Finally, there has existed a strong bias that only texts can inform us adequately on religious matters—that philology, rather than the study of material remains, should prevail. Yet archaeology is forcing us to revise our basic perception of ancient

Israelite popular religion. Virtually expunged from the texts of the Hebrew Bible and all but forgotten by rabbinical times, folk religion enjoyed a vigorous life throughout the monarchy. This is not really surprising, since most Bible scholars now agree that true monotheism (not merely henotheism, the worship of one god without denying the existence of other gods) arose only in the period of the Exile or later.[26]

Even during the period of true monotheism, the popular cult survived. There are reflexes of the cult of the old mother goddess in later Judaism, such as the personification of divine Wisdom (Sophia) and the conception of the Shekinah, or effective presence of the divine in the world, which medieval texts of the Jewish Kabbalist sect sometimes called the "Bride of God."[27] Similarly, certain Christian doctrines may derive from a primitive memory of feminine manifestations of the deity; this can be seen in the development of the doctrine of the Holy Spirit—a more immanent, nurturing aspect of the transcendent God. Perhaps, too, the image of Asherah dimly survives in the elevation of Mary to "Mother of God," a feminine intermediary to whom many less "sophisticated" Christians pray. In both Jewish and Christian circles, the main-stream, orthodox clergy has resisted these "pagan" influences, supporting instead rigorously monotheistic doctrines. But in popular religion, the old cults die hard. And when they finally do, archaeology may help to resurrect them.

THE RELIGIOUS REFORMS
OF HEZEKIAH AND JOSIAH

P. Kyle McCarter, Jr

The religious reforms of Kings Hezekiah (727-698 B.C.E.) and Josiah (639-608 B.C.E.) of Judah occurred at a time when other Near Eastern civilizations were also carrying out reforms aimed at reviving classical beliefs and traditions.[1]

In Egypt, one manifestation of this neoclassical spirit is the so-called Shabaka Stone. Pharaoh Shabaka (716-695 B.C.E.) ruled during the XXVth Dynasty, while Egypt was under the domination of Nubia (southern Egypt and the Sudan today). Nubia had long been heavily Egyptianized, and the Nubians promoted traditional Egyptian values derived from the cult of Amun, established by Pharaoh Thutmose III (1479-1425 B.C.E.) in the upper Nile. Shabaka is said to have discovered a stone with text copied from an ancient papyrus manuscript—"a work of the ancestors which was worm-eaten, so that it could not be understood from beginning to end."[2] The original text purportedly contained ancient Memphite theological and cosmological ideas to be revived and promulgated in eighth- and seventh-century B.C.E. Egypt.

The recovery of the Shabaka Stone has a curious parallel in Judah, where another ancient document was found and used to propagate an older, more traditional set of religious beliefs. During the reign of Josiah, according to 2 Kings 22:8, the priest Hilkiah found a book containing Mosaic teachings "in the house of Yahweh," the Jerusalem Temple. King Josiah is reported to have used this "book of the Torah"—which many scholars believe to have been an early form of the Book of Deuteronomy—as the basis of his religious reforms. It is Deuteronomy, and the literature associated with it, that provides our earliest textual evidence of a developed monotheism.

The Deuteronomic Revolution

In Judah, this international neoclassicism expressed itself in an ongoing reform movement that waxed and waned from the late eighth to the early sixth centuries B.C.E. This movement peaked during the reigns of Hezekiah and Josiah and left its permanent expression in the Deuteronomic literature (the Book of Deuteronomy plus the books of Joshua, Judges, Samuel and Kings). According to 2 Chronicles 29-32, Hezekiah began his reform in the first year of his reign; motivated by the belief that the ancient religion was not being practiced scrupulously, he ordered that the Temple of Yahweh be repaired and cleansed of *niddâ* (impurity). After celebrating a truly national Passover for the first time since the reign of Solomon (2 Chronicles 30:26), Hezekiah's officials went into the countryside and dismantled the local shrines or "high places" (*bamot*) along with their altars, "standing stones" (*masseboth*) and "sacred poles" (*'ăšērîm*).

The Shabaka Stone. This basalt slab, measuring about 3 feet by 5.5 feet, was carved at the behest of King Shabaka (716-695 B.C.E.), the first ruler of Egypt's XXVth Dynasty (the Nubian dynasty). The text on the stone purports to be a copy of an ancient composition describing the creation of the world by the Memphite god Ptah. Shabaka's attempt to revive an ancient theology has a parallel in Israel, where an old book of Moses' teachings (2 Kings 22:8) was found during the reign of King Josiah (639-608 B.C.E.). This book was probably Deuteronomy, which was then used by Josiah to carry out his religious reforms.

The account of Hezekiah's reform activities in 2 Kings 18:1-8 is much briefer. Although he is credited with removing the high places, the major reform is credited to Josiah (2 Kings 22:3–23:25). Since Chronicles is a much later source than Kings—and, in fact, often draws openly on both the narrative and language of Kings—historians normally give preference to Kings over Chronicles when there is a discrepancy between them or a difference of emphasis. But in this case there are good reasons to accept the viewpoint of the Chronicler. The Kings account was probably written by a historian commissioned by Josiah,[3] who would have emphasized the contribution of his royal patron. Archaeology, moreover, has shown that many of the civil and political changes associated with the centralization of the cult in Jerusalem probably took place during Hezekiah's reign, when Jerusalem itself underwent a major expansion. Nahman Avigad's 1970 excavation in the Jewish Quarter, for example, exposed a 20-foot-thick wall dating to this period—evidently the new wall Hezekiah built outside the old city wall (2 Chronicles 32:5). This westward expansion of the city must have been intended, at least in part, to accommodate refugees from the fall of Samaria (Israel) to the Assyrians in 721 B.C.E; and the wall discovered by Avigad must have been built in anticipation of Sennacherib's 701 B.C.E. invasion, as the Chronicles account makes clear. The vitality of Hezekiah's administration is further illustrated by excavations throughout Judah.[4]

Thus archaeology provides evidence of a burgeoning, centralized Judahite state during the period of the reforms reported in Kings and Chronicles, and it shows that the centralization began with Hezekiah. But it does not provide direct evidence of religious reform activities, which are much harder to identify in the archaeological record.

When, for example, were the high places removed? On this score, there is little reason to doubt the biblical account that they were dismantled during the reigns of both Hezekiah and Josiah. We even have some archaeological evidence. At Arad, in the Negev desert, excavator Yohanan Aharoni found a small temple that seems to have been roughly contemporary with Solomon's Temple. This discovery, along with the recovery of sacrificial altars from other Judahite sites such as Beersheba, shows that animal sacrifice was indeed offered at high places *(bamot)* during the period before the reforms. According to Aharoni, the altar of the Arad temple went out of use at the end of the eighth century B.C.E. and the entire shrine was abandoned late in the seventh century B.C.E.—changes that Aharoni attributed to the reforms of Hezekiah and then Josiah. Although reevaluation of the archaeological evidence from Arad suggests that the temple continued in use during the final

"Belonging to the king" (lmlk) *is inscribed on both of these stamps from late-eighth-century B.C.E. ceramic storage jar handles. The* lmlk *stamps are part of a large corpus of evidence indicating the existence of an expanding state in Judah during the reign of Hezekiah. This nation-building activity also included the centralization of Israelite religion; Hezekiah sought to centralize the worship of the Israelite God Yahweh in Jerusalem by tearing down outlying shrines and destroying images of Yahweh and other deities.*

phase of the fortress (the early sixth century B.C.E.), there remain indications that the temple was dismantled before the destruction of the site. The temple's two small altars, probably for burning incense, were carefully laid on their sides and covered with plaster, apparently in an attempt to cancel out Arad's high place in the course of Josiah's reform.

This elimination of local places of worship is very important to the early development of Jewish monotheism. On the surface, the issue at stake seems be purely cultic, having much to do with where and how the god of Israel should be worshiped and little to do with his divine nature. But another aspect of the matter

ZEEV MESHEL

"Yahweh of Teman." Like the pithos *fragment shown on page 43, this pottery sherd from Kuntillet ʿAjrud contains a blessing: "I bless you by Yahweh of Teman and by his Asherah." Blessings found elsewhere use similar phrasing—referring, for example, to Yahweh of Samaria or to Yahweh of Hebron. Although most Israelites probably believed in only one god (Yahweh), that god sometimes had local manifestations that could become quasi-independent— attenuating the idea of a single, universal deity. The religious reforms of the eighth and seventh centuries B.C.E. were presumably intended, in part, to combat this tendency to multiply Yahwehs.*

deserves consideration. Once again, archaeology has supplied essential information—in the form of eighth-century B.C.E. Hebrew inscriptions found at Kuntillet ʿAjrud, on the Sinai peninsula. Before the discovery of these inscriptions, we had no pre-reform-period Hebrew text with any extensive religious content. When the ʿAjrud materials were read, however, they proved to be substantially religious in content, and they have provided important information about pre-reform Israelite religion during the Iron Age, much of which we have only begun to appreciate. Especially significant for the issue of cult centralization is the fact that in the ʿAjrud texts the God of Israel is not referred to simply as Yahweh but, in every unbroken context, as "Yahweh of GN" (with GN standing for a geographical name). In particular, we have "Yahweh of Samaria" (*yhwh šmrn*) and "Yahweh of Teman" (*yhwh htmn* in the dialect of the northern kingdom of Israel, and *yhwh htymn* in the dialect of the southern kingdom of Judah). The Yahweh of Samaria was the local form, or manifestation, of

Yahweh as he was worshiped in the capital of the northern king-dom (Israel). The Yahweh of Teman, or of "the Southland," was presumably the local Yahweh of the area around Kuntillet ʿAjrud—biblical Teman was a region, not a city,[5] and Kuntillet ʿAjrud is known in Hebrew as Horvat Teman, the ruins of Teman.

"Yahweh of Samaria" and "Yahweh of Teman" belong to a cat-egory of divine name well known outside Israel. These names take the form "DN of GN," where DN is a divine name or national god and GN is a geographical name, designating a particular local shrine or temple where the god or goddess was worshiped. The great Mesopotamian goddess Ishtar, for example, had principal cult centers in the Assyrian cities of Nineveh and Arbela. Although every pious Assyrian knew there was only one Ishtar, prayers and sacrifices were offered to Ishtar of Nineveh or Ishtar of Arbela. When the Assyrian king Assurbanipal (668-627 B.C.E.) or one of his royal predecessors called upon the Assyrian gods to sanction a treaty, he was careful to invoke both Ishtar of Nineveh and Ishtar of Arbela, as if "Ishtar" alone would have been insufficient. This shows that local manifestations of a god, when approached in the cult for purposes of worship, tended to become quasi-independent.

This was also true concerning local manifestations of Yahweh, as illustrated by an episode in the story of Absalom's revolt in 2 Samuel 15. Following his murder of his brother Amnon, Absalom flees to the land of Geshur in the modern Golan Heights and then returns to Jerusalem and surrenders to David. After four years of house arrest in Jerusalem, he approaches the king with the following request: "Let me go fulfill the vow I made to Yahweh in Hebron (*yhwh bhbrwn*), for your servant made a vow when I was living in Aram-geshur, as follows: 'If Yahweh will bring me back to Jerusalem, I shall serve Yahweh!'" (2 Samuel 15:7-8). The phrase "to Yahweh in Hebron" cannot be read as indicating the place where the vow was made, since Absalom says he made it in Geshur. Instead, the words "in Hebron" qualify "Yahweh"; it is to

Israelite Monarchies
in Iron Age I (1000-586 B.C.E.)
United Monarchy
David c. 1000-961
Solomon c. 961-921

Divided Monarchy

Kingdom of Judah		*Kingdom of Israel*	
Rehoboam	921-913	Jeroboam I	921-910
Abijam (Abijah)	913-911		
Asa	911-869		
		Nadab	910-909
		Baasha	909-886
		Elah	886-885
		Zimn	885
Jehoshaphat	872-848		
		Omri	885-874
		Ahab	874-853
		Ahaziah	853-852
Jehoram	854-841	Joram	852-841
Ahaziah	841		
Athaliah	841-835	Jehu	841-814
Jehoash	835-796	Jehoahaz	814-798
Amaziah	796-790	Joash	798-782
		Jeroboam II	793-753
Uzziah (Azariah)	790-739		
		Zachariah	753-752
		Shallum	752
Jotham	750-731	Menahem	752-742
		Pekahiah	742-740
Ahaz	735-715	Pekah	740-732
		Hoshea	732-723/722
Hezekiah	**727-698**		
Manasseh	696-641		
Amon	641-639		
Josiah	**639-608**		
Jehoahaz	608		
Jehoiakim	608-598		
Jehoiachin	598-597		
Zedekiah	597-586		

the Hebronite Yahweh that Absalom owes a votive gift—hence his request to make the trip.

Local cults, therefore, had the potential to become powerful and independent even if they were not centers for the worship of foreign gods. The elimination of the high places and the centralization of the cult in Jerusalem put an end to the authority not only of the local priesthoods but also of the local Yahwehs. For this reason, the theology of the Deuteronomic literature is sometimes referred to as "MonoYahwism," and the danger posed by the quasi-independent local Yahwehs helps explain one of the most important passages in this literature. Deuteronomy 6:4-5 provides the opening verses of the *Shema* (Deuteronomy 6:4-9) in Jewish tradition and the Great Commandment (see Mark 12:29-30) in Christianity:

> *šĕmaʿ yiśrāʾēl yhwh ʾĕlōhênû yhwh ʾeḥād wĕʾāhabtā ʾēt yhwh ʾĕlōhêkā bĕkol-lĕbābĕkā ûbĕkol-napšĕkā ûbĕkol-mĕʾōdékā.*
>
> Hear, O Israel! Yahweh our god, Yahweh is one! And you shall love Yahweh your god with all your heart and with all your soul and with all your might!

Verse 5, which requires that the Israelites' religious devotion and energy be directed exclusively towards Yahweh, draws on the common "love" language of ancient Near Eastern political loyalty.[6] This is love that can be commanded—political loyalty and exclusive allegience.

The passage continues in this vein in Deuteronomy 6:13-15:

> It is Yahweh your god whom you shall fear, and it is he whom you shall serve, and it is in his name that you shall swear. You shall not go after other gods from the gods of the nations that are around you—since Yahweh your god who is in your midst is a jealous god (*ʾēl qannāʾ*)—lest the anger of Yahweh your god be ignited against you and exterminate you from the land.

The penalty for the worship of other gods is exile—"from the face of the land" (*whišmīdĕkā mēʿal pĕnê hāʾădāmâ*)—not from the face of the earth. This threat of exile, made explicit with the same language in Deuteronomy 28:63–64a (compare 28:48), comes at the climax of a long list of curses warning against disobeying the Deuteronomic laws: "Just as Yahweh exulted over you when he was doing good for you and multiplying you, so Yahweh will exult over you when he causes you to perish and exterminates you and tears you out of the land which he gave you to possess and scatters you among the nations from one end of the earth to the other." These passages, written down at a time when mere threats had become a grim reality, interpret the destruction of Jerusalem in 586 B.C.E. and the ensuing Babylonian Exile as punishment for Israel's failure to worship Yahweh exclusively.

Yahweh exacts this punishment because he is "a jealous god" (*ʾēl qannāʾ*). This phrase is used in Deuteronomy almost as if it were a technical term for a god who will not share his worship with other gods. The central passage is the text of the Second Commandment, as reckoned in Jewish tradition:

> You shall have no other gods before me. You shall not make yourselves an idol—the form of anything in the sky above or in the earth below or in the waters that are under the earth. You shall not bow down to them or serve them, for I, Yahweh your god, am a jealous god (*ʾēl qannāʾ*), visiting the sins of the fathers upon the sons to the third and fourth generation for those who hate me, and dealing loyally by the thousands with those who love me and keep my commandments.

> Deuteronomy 5:7-10//Exodus 20:3-6

The meaning of *ʾēl qannāʾ* is not that Yahweh is such a *zealous* god that he holds multiple generations responsible for sin* but

*The JPS translation incorrectly renders this phrase as "an impassioned god."

that he is *jealous;* he is so intolerant of the worship of other gods and especially of idols that he will punish "those who hate him" (the apostates) and reward "those who love him."

The issue at stake here is not MonoYahwism. Nor is it exactly what we consider monotheism, the denial of the existence of other gods. What the passages espouse is monolatry—confinement of worship to a single god—which includes a strong component of aniconism, the repudiation of any visual representation of deity. We are thus led to ask, To what extent was Israelite religion before the reform period polylatrous and representational? That is, did Israelites worship many gods and represent them with icons or idols? The easy answer to this question is yes. The biblical writers report that they did, and the archaeological record confirms it. But on closer inspection the answer turns out to be somewhat less straightforward.

The Origins of Monotheism

Older models generally described the origins of monotheism as following an evolutionary pattern. In the 19th century it seemed reasonable to suppose that human religion tended to evolve in stages. It began in primitive societies as a kind of spirit worship, sometimes called polydemonism; with the rise of complex societies, it developed into polytheism, the belief in an organized pantheon of gods; eventually, polytheism was replaced by monotheism, the ideal and perhaps inevitable goal of developed religion. These idealized schemes were discredited in the early 20th century, when anthropologists began to visit so-called primitive societies and to discover that some of them, though at a neolithic stage of material culture, were in fact monotheistic and showed no sign of ever having been anything else.

The history of ancient Near Eastern religions suggests that the same people sometimes see the divine as singular and sometimes as plural. Most monotheistic religions have at least some plural ways of viewing their god—who may act through angels or humans with superhuman powers—and yet remain committed to the belief that there is one god. Similarly, polytheistic religions often find monotheistic expressions. There is an often-cited hymn to the Mesopotamian god Ninurta, for example, in which a worshiper who surely believes in the independent reality of each member of the pantheon nevertheless identifies many of the great gods and goddesses with parts of Ninurta's body:

> Warlike Ninurta ...
> Your face is Shamash [the sun god],
> Your two eyes, lord, are Enlil [the lord of the earth]
>   and Ninlil [his consort] ...
> The iris of your eye, lord, is ... Sin [the moon god] ...
> The lashes of your eyes are the rays of Shamash.
> The form of your mouth, lord, is Ishtar of the stars.
> Anu [the god who presides in the divine assembly]
>   and Antu [his consort] are your two lips,
>   your command ...
> Your teeth are the Sibitti [the seven ruling gods], who
>   overthrow the wicked.
> Your two ears, O speaker of wisdom, are Ea and
>   Damkina [god and goddess of wisdom].
> Your head is Adad [the rain god], who shapes heaven
>   and earth like a master craftsman.

Or consider this hymn to the goddess Baba, which identifies her with female deities worshiped in different local cults:

> In Ur you are Ningal, the sister of the great gods.
> In Ekishshirgal ... you are Ningiazagga, the
>   protectress of all mankind, the light of the
>   high heavens.
> In Sippar, the ancient city, the light of heaven and
>   earth, of gods and men, you are, in [the temple]

Eababarra, [the goddess] Aa ...
In Ehili, you are Ishtar ...
In Babylon, the gathering place of the gods, you
are Ninahakuddu.
In Esagila, you are Eru'a, who creates offerings ...

Perhaps the best known of these texts is a god-list that identifies the major male deities as aspects of Marduk, god of Babylon, relating to their functions:

Urash (is)	Marduk of planting.
Ninurta (is)	Marduk of the pickaxe.
Nergal (is)	Marduk of battle.
Zababa (is)	Marduk of warfare.
Enlil (is)	Marduk of lordship and consultations.
Nabû (is)	Marduk of accounting.
Sin (is)	Marduk who lights up the light.
Shamash (is)	Marduk of justice.
Adad (is)	Marduk of rain.

Another well-known phenomenon in world religions helps explain how a single god can generate other gods. This is the phenomenon of hypostasis, according to which some property of a deity, such as his anger or wisdom or cultic presence, is considered an entity in itself and in some cases is personified. In biblical and early postbiblical Judaism and in early Christianity, the wisdom of God is hypostatized. Thus in Proverb 9:1-4a the *ḥokmâ*, or wisdom of God, is presented in hypostatic form:

Wisdom has built her house,
    she has hewn her seven pillars,
She has slaughtered her animals, mixed her wine.
    Yes, she has set her table.
She has sent out her young women,
    she calls from the rooftops of the city,
"Whoever is foolish, turn aside here!"

Mary, mother of Jesus, *is depicted on the* Altarpiece of the Lamb, *in the Cathedral of Saint Bavo, in Ghent, Belgium—completed by Jan Van Eyck in about 1432. In the Israelite cult and in later Judaism, the single, universal and invisible Yahweh was sometimes worshiped through one or several of his aspects: for example, through the concept of his presence (what the early rabbis called the Shekinah) or that of his name. Another aspect of God, his wisdom, appears in the Hebrew Bible personified as Lady Wisdom (Proverbs 1-9). In Christianity, Mary was sometimes identified as the Wisdom of God (or as Sophia, which means wisdom in Greek) and thus is often portrayed, as in the Ghent Altarpiece, holding an open book.*

Lady Wisdom is very prominent in Jewish literature; we encounter her in Proverbs 1-9, Job 28, Ben Sira 24 and the Wisdom of Solomon. In early Christianity, she was known by her Greek name, Sophia. In Gnostic texts, she appears as the mother or consort of a number of divine beings. In non-Gnostic Christianity, she is linked closely with Jesus Christ, in a male-female complementarity that recalled her origin as an aspect of God. This is expressed icono-graphically in a painting on the doorway of the catacomb of Karmouz at Alexandria, where an angel with wings is designated "Sophia Jesus Christ." Similarly, one of a pair of Coptic reliquary crosses displaying identical figures is labeled "Jesus Christ," while the other is labeled "Mother Christ." In the great church of Hagia Sophia in Istanbul and elsewhere, Wisdom was subsumed under the representation of Mary, as shown by her portrayal in the apse of Santa Sophia in Kiev. In a 14th-century tapestry, Mary is depicted as Athena, the wise goddess who sprang fully grown from the head of Zeus; she and her suppliant wear similiar crowns, and the book they both hold is an invincible shield illustrating the text of Wisdom of Solomon 7:30: "Against Wisdom evil does not prevail." Almost the same iconography appears in Jan Van Eyck's elegant portrait of Mary as Lady Wisdom in the Ghent Altarpiece.

Except in Gnosticism, the hypostatization of Lady Wisdom in Judaism and Christianity probably never reached the point where she was fully personified as a goddess. This is not true, however, in other ancient cases of hypostasis. In the fourth-century B.C.E. Jewish colony on Elephantine Island in Upper Egypt, for example, Yahweh—or Yahu, as they called him—was worshiped under the surrogate name Bethel, or "House of God." Offerings were made, however, not only to Yahu or Bethel but also to at least three other deities whose names originally denoted aspects of the cultic presence of Yahu: Herem-Bethel ("the Sacredness of Bethel," that is, "the Sacredness of Yahu"), Eshem-Bethel ("the Name of Bethel") and Anath-Bethel, also called Anath-Yahu. The last name probably

"YHW, the God dwelling in Yeb" reads the outlined text in this fourth-century B.C.E. papyrus document from the island of Elephantine in the Nile River. The Elephantine Jewish community apparently worshiped the local Yahweh, who resided in Yeb, an Egyptian word meaning Elephant Land. Other documents from the site suggest that the inhabitants also worshiped different aspects of their local Yahweh: his House (or dwelling-place); his Sacredness; and his Sign (or active presence).

means "the Sign of Yahu," that is, the visible sign of the cultic presence of Yahu. In Elephantine Judaism, then, at least three aspects of Yahweh—his Sacredness, his Name and his Active Sign—were hypostatized, personified and worshiped as deities.

The evidence from the history of religions suggests, therefore, that polytheism and monotheism are not ideal, exclusive religious patterns, and that the development of one into the other cannot be predicted, though it can be observed and described. Nor does Jewish monotheism seem to have arisen out of a form of polytheism similar to that which prevailed in Mesopotamia or in Late Bronze Age Syria and Canaan. Instead, at the beginning of the Iron Age (around 1200 B.C.E.), a different religious pattern appeared among the new and larger nation-states that emerged in Syria-Palestine.

In the religions of the Late Bronze Age (about 1550-1200 B.C.E.), each city-state seems to have had a principal deity—like Ba'al Zaphon of Ugarit—who was preeminent in the esteem of the citizens and whose favor and protection were regarded as essential to the welfare of the state. This deity, however, was perceived as only the foremost of a number of deities—some of whom had their own temples standing alongside that of the major god. In the religions of the new Iron Age nation-states, on the other hand, the preeminent city god was replaced by a supreme national god, who, as far as our evidence permits us to say, was almost the sole object of worship in the community.

We know the names of these national gods from the Bible and from epigraphic materials found in Israel, Jordan and Syria. They included, among others, Milcom the god of Ammon, Chemosh the god of Moab, Qos the god of Edom and Yahweh the god of Israel. A theological rationale for the division of the land into nation-states worshiping national gods is recorded in Deuteronomy 32:8-9, the original form of which is preserved in the Greek Bible and a manuscript from Qumran:

> When the Most High apportioned the nations,
>   when he divided up the sons of man,
> He established the boundaries of the peoples,
>   according to the number of the sons of God.
> The allotment of Yahweh was his people,
>   Jacob was his portion of the estate.

And we can add that the Ammonites were the allotment of Milcom, the Moabites the allotment of Chemosh and so on.

As Israelite religion developed at the close of the Iron Age, and then passed through the extraordinary period of religious creativity that transformed it from pre-Exilic Yahwism into early Judaism, the Most High God of Deuteronomy 32:8 was exclusively identified with Yahweh. And with the emergence of Jewish monotheism, the power of the other gods, and eventually their very existence, was denied.

But even within the earlier nation-state formulation of the Iron Age, official Israelite religion showed little interest in other gods or goddesses. In the onomastic records from that period— that is, the lists of surviving personal names—citizens of Israel and its neighboring nation-states bore names that commonly included as a theophoric element the name of their national god or the generic name *ʾēl*, simply "god"; but these names almost never included a theophoric element associated with any other god. Moreover, the oldest literature preserved in the Bible, together with the scant corpus of texts that archaeologists have recovered from the Syro-Palestinian nation-states of the Iron Age, suggests that the divine was perceived as an essential singularity, with significant historical events being attributed to the will of the national god and no other. In the inscription of the ninth-century B.C.E. Moabite king Mesha, for example, Moab's domination by Israel during the reign of Omri is attributed not to the superior power of the Israelite god, or to the interplay of human forces, but to the fact that "Chemosh was angry with his land," a theological interpretation of national hardship that has clear parallels in the Bible.

Yahweh and His Asherah

The predominant pattern of Iron Age religion in the nation-states of Syria-Palestine was, if not truly monotheistic, at least monolatrous—confining worship to a single god—and henotheistic—viewing the world in terms of the will of a single god without necessarily denying the existence of others. But if in the Iron Age the worship of a single god had already become predominant, what is the point of the "jealous god" motif of Deuteronomy and the reform movements? The injunction

Yahweh established nations by drawing up boundaries "according to the number of the sons of God" (Deuteronomy 32:8). On this Dead Sea Scroll fragment of Deuteronomy 32:8 appear the words "sons of God" (in the rabbinic text, the wording is "sons of Israel," probably a rabbinic emendation). The biblical

text thus conceives of a number of nation-states, with each devoted to its own national god. The god of Edom, for example, is Qos (which we know from inscriptions), while the god of Israel is Yahweh.

against worshiping foreign gods is clear enough, insisting on sole allegience to the national god. But the principal stricture in the "jealous god" passage involves the prohibition of cultic representations, or idol worship; and the accounts of Hezekiah's and Josiah's reform activities stress not only the removal of high places, but also the destruction of *masseboth* and *ăšērîm*.

Masseboth, we know, are standing stones erected to signify divine presence.* But what is an asherah?

The term "asherah" appears many times in the Bible. In 1 Kings 15:13, we are told that the eighth-century B.C.E. king Asa deposed his mother, Maacah, as Queen Mother of Judah "because she had made a *mipleṣet* for Asherah. Asa cut down her *mipleṣet* and burned it in the Kidron Valley." The obscure Hebrew term *mipleṣet* is apparently to be understood as "a horrible thing," the

---

*This is clear from the story of Jacob's ladder in Genesis 28:10-22, in which Jacob, having discovered in a dream that the spot where he slept possessed a staircase connecting heaven and earth, erected the stone he had used as a pillow as a *massebah* (28:18) and declared the place to be "Bethel, the House of God" (28:22).

original word possibly having meant something like "hewn, carved image."[7] But who is Asherah, for whom the image was hewn? We know Asherah from many sources as the name of a Canaanite and Syrian goddess: the Ugaritic Asherah, or Athiratu (*ʾṯrt*), figures prominently in Ugaritic myth. Accordingly, we might assume with past generations of scholarship that the Asherah worshiped in Judah was a foreign goddess and that the cult of eighth-century B.C.E. Jerusalem was syncretistic.

But that assumption is probably wrong, given the monolatrous character of pre-reform Yahwism. A more likely explanation is suggested by the inscriptions and graffiti discovered at Kuntillet ʿAjrud. A number of these texts contain divine blessings invoked "by Yahweh ... and his asherah" (*lyhwh ... wlʾšrth*). Note especially that asherah, whoever or whatever she or it is, is described as Yahweh's asherah. In the Bible, the term asherah refers not only to a goddess, Asherah, but also to a wooden cult object, an asherah, and some evidence suggests that the term might also mean "shrine." Thus the expression "Yahweh's asherah" might refer to a cult object or shrine associated with the worship of Yahweh. Even if this is the case, however, the structure of the blessing formula shows that the asherah—whatever it refers to primarily—had a kind of personality, which is invoked for blessing alongside Yahweh.

So we return to the idea of hypostasis, in which abstract aspects of a god are attributed concrete substance and worshiped as partly or entirely independent deities. As is common among the religions of ancient Syria and Canaan, some abstract aspect of a god might be attributed substantial form and personified as *female*. Thus there was a group of female deities who seem to have arisen as hypostatic forms of leading male deities. Each of these goddesses was given an epithet that identified her as the Face or Name of the god, that is, as his cultic presence. Thus in the Late Bronze Age, for example, the Ugaritic goddess Ashtart was called "Name-of-Baʿal" (*ʿṯtrt šm bʿl*), an epithet that was still used of the Sidonian Ashtart (*ʿštrt šm bʿl*) eight centuries later. Similarly, the great goddess Tannith, who was worshiped at the Phoenician colony of Carthage, was identified as *tnt pn b'l*—the Face or Presence of the chief Punic god, Ba'al Hammon—as she is called on a typical votive stela from Tunis with its aniconic representation of the goddess Tannith.

The male deity is the community's chief god, whose favor and sustenance are essential to its welfare. The female deity is the male deity's consort, but she arises as a hypostatic form of his Face or Name, that is, of his cultic presence. The religious issue is that of cultic presence and availability, an issue classically expressed in the study of religion as the theological problem of divine transcendence and immanence. How can a great god, who transcends the ordinary world, be said to be immanent in an earthly temple? Solomon expressed the anxiety associated with this problem in his prayer dedicating the Temple: "Will a god really dwell on earth? The heavens and the heavens' heavens cannot contain you, much less this house that I have built!" (1 Kings 8:27). The solution offered in 1 Kings is that although Yahweh will continue to dwell in heaven, his *Name* will dwell in the Temple in Jerusalem. When prayers and petitions are brought to Yahweh's Name on earth, Yahweh himself will hear them in heaven. Solomon expresses this idea in the continuation of his prayer:

> Turn your face towards your servant and his supplication, O Yahweh my god, hearing the cry and the prayer that your servant is praying in your presence today, so that your eyes may be open to this house night and day and to this place of which you have said, "Let my name be there!" so that you might hear the prayer that your servant prays in this place. Hear the cry of your servant and your people which they pray in this place, so that you might hear in your dwelling place in heaven, and hearing forgive.

> 1 Kings 8:28-30

Tree of Life? *The* pithos *from eighth-century B.C.E. Kuntillet ʿAjrud shown on page 43 also contains a drawing (see reconstruction) of a tree flanked by ibexes above a lion. The accompanying text solicits a blessing from "Yahweh ... and his Asherah." The term "asherah" appears many times in the Hebrew Bible. Sometimes asherah refers to an anthropomorphic deity (2 Kings 23:4), probably related to the Canaanite goddess Asherah (who was often associated with lions). Elsewhere in the Bible, asherah is described as a wooden cult object—a sacred pole or a tree (1 Kings 14:23). In either case, pre-reform Israelite cults often conceived of a quasi-divine entity in association with their national god, Yahweh.*

We do not know how far the hypostatization, personification and deification of the divine presence went in ancient Israel. In the Bible, the Name and Presence of God are given hypostatic form, but they are not personified except, notably, in the form of *malʾākîm*, "messengers" or "angels." In postbiblical Judaism, the Presence of God was hypostatized as the Shekinah (*šĕkînâ*), the indwelling or attentive cultic presence of God. According to *Sifre Numbers* 94, God placed his Shekinah in the midst of the Israelites, so that, according to *Baba Bathra* 25a, "to whatever place they were exiled, the Shekinah went with them." According to other Talmudic pronouncements, the Shekinah was everywhere (*Roš Hašana*); it was, for instance, always present above a sick person's bed (*Šabbath* 30a; *Pesaḥ* 117a). In the Midrash *mišlê* on Proverb 22:8, the personification of the Shekinah has proceeded far enough that she is presented as speaking to God. And in the *Sefer ha-Bahir*, the earliest Kabbalistic work, she is called Daughter, Princess, *Malkût*. In Kabbalistic philosophy, the Shekinah is the feminine principle in the world of the divine *sĕfîrôt*: the ten primordial or ideal "numbers," of which the *šĕkînâ* is the tenth, which emanated from God and created the world—creation and revelation proceed through her.

Yahweh's asherah, as known from the inscriptions "to Yahweh and his Asherah" on *pithoi* from Kuntillet ʿAjrud, should be understood in the same way as the Anath-Yahu of Elephantine Judaism or the Name and Face of Baʿal goddesses of the Phoenician and Punic world. The verb from which the Hebrew word *ăšērâ* is derived (√*ṯr) means "pass along; leave a trace, leave a mark," and the basic meaning of *ăšērâ* was probably something like "track, trace, sign, mark, vestige," or perhaps "effect, influence"—resembling the Arabic *ʾaṯar*. Yahweh's *ăšērâ*, then, was a palpable mark of his effective influence. The term is often used in the Bible, as noted earlier, to refer to a wooden cult object, probably a simple wooden pole but possibly even a sacred tree, which served as part of a shrine and concretely represented Yahweh's availability for worship. When this mark of Yahweh's presence was hypostatized and attributed a feminine personality, it came to be thought of as a deity, a goddess.

On one *pithos* from Kuntillet ʿAjrud, two figures are depicted in the foreground (see photo, p. 43). Some scholars have interpreted these figures as a pair of representations of the Egyptian god Bes. But that is not so; the figures in fact represent Yahweh and his Asherah, as the blessing written over the depiction suggests. This is the Samarian Yahweh, depicted in human form with a bull's head, hooves and a tail—the "young bull of Samaria" condemned in Hosea 8:5-6 and elsewhere. His Asherah, who also has bovine horns, hooves and a crown, stands alongside him in the conventional position of the consort in, for example, Egyptian art. She is a goddess, but she is a Yahwistic goddess, not a Canaanite goddess. She represents Yahweh's presence, just as the wooden pole that she personifies represents it in his shrine. It was this iconography that the Deuteronomic reforms deplored and attempted to eradicate: the representation of Yahweh as a bull, the representation of his available presence as a goddess and the cultic representation of both by *masseboth* and *ʾăšērîm*.

These changes, together with the eradication of local places of worship and the revival of Israel's ancient distrust of foreign gods, led to an aniconic and nonlocalized form of Yahwism. In turn, this form of Yahwism led, in the years of the Exile and thereafter, to the development of a more abstract and rigidly aniconic form of monotheism than the Israelites had known in the pre-reform period.

JEWISH MONOTHEISM
AND CHRISTIAN THEOLOGY

✝

John J. Collins

"In the beginning was the Word" reads the opening verse of the Gospel of John, "and the Word was with God, and the Word was God." In the context of the gospel, it is clear that the Word is identified with Jesus of Nazareth, the charismatic preacher who had been crucified by the Romans some 60 years before the gospel was written. John's gospel is exceptional in the New Testament for the explicitness of its claim that Jesus was divine. Nonetheless, it is both the culmination of a trend within Judaism and a good indicator of the course Christian theology would take in the following centuries. This development would accentuate the gap between emerging Christianity and Judaism.

By nearly all accounts, at the end of the first century C.E. strict monotheism had long been one of the pillars of Judaism.[1]

John takes pains to show how unacceptable Jesus' claim of divinity was to Jews: "For this reason the Jews were seeking all the more to kill him, because he was not only breaking the Sabbath, but was also calling God his own Father, thereby making himself equal to God" (John 5:18). This gospel is traditionally attributed to one of the Jewish disciples of Jesus. Even though that attribution is problematic, the Christian movement had unquestionably originated in the heart of Judaism little more than half a century earlier. Yet, in the opinion of one modern scholar, John's version of a divine Jesus is so elevated that observant Jews at the beginning of the first century C.E.—including the first apostles—could not have believed in such a figure.[2] The question is, How was it possible for first-century C.E. Jews to accept this man Jesus as the pre-existent Son of God and still believe, as they surely did, that they were not violating traditional Jewish monotheism? How did this development come about?

Was Judaism Monotheistic?

Jewish monotheism, which gave birth to the Christian movement, was not as clear cut and simple as is generally believed. Several kinds of quasi-divine figures appear in Jewish texts from the Hellenistic period that seem to call for some qualification of the idea of monotheism. We will consider three categories of such figures—angels or demigods, exalted human beings and the more abstract figures of Wisdom and the Word (Logos).[3]

Angelic figures. The latest book of the Hebrew Bible contains a passage that had great significance for early Christians. In the Book of Daniel, the visionary sees that "thrones were set in place and an Ancient One took his throne, his clothing was white as snow, and the hair of his head like pure wool; his throne was fiery flames, and its wheels were burning fire" (Daniel 7:9). The Ancient One is the God of Israel, even though some of his features, like his

Daniel envisions "one like a son of man" given "an everlasting dominion" by God (Daniel 7:13-14)—*in this illumination from a 12th-century C.E. edition of a commentary on the Apocalypse by the 8th-century Spanish monk Beatus of Liebana. The Book of Daniel (mid-second century B.C.E.) is one of a number of apocalyptic Jewish texts from the Hellenistic period in which semidivine figures appear alongside Yahweh. Later, in early Christianity, Jesus was to be identified as the Son of Man. The existence of such angelic or quasi-divine beings asks us to reflect on what is meant by the term "monotheism."*

white hair, are reminiscent of the ancient Canaanite god El. The ancient rabbis were troubled by the plural term "thrones," which indicates that at least one other figure will be enthroned. Indeed, a second figure makes his entrance a few verses later:

> I saw one like a son of man
>   coming with the clouds of heaven.
> And he came to the Ancient One
>   and was presented before him.
> To him was given dominion
>   and glory and kingship,
> that all peoples, nations and languages
>   should serve him.
> His dominion is an everlasting dominion
>   that shall not pass away,
> and his kingship is one
>   that shall never be destroyed.
>
> Daniel 7:13-14

Monotheistic theologians commonly interpret the "one like a son of man" as a symbol for Israel.[4] The figure does indeed represent Israel in some sense, but the manner in which he is presented cannot be brushed aside so lightly.[5] Elsewhere in the Hebrew Bible, a figure riding on the clouds is always the Lord, the God of Israel.* Daniel's imagery has its background in ancient Canaanite mythology, in which the god Ba'al rides the clouds and is distinct from the venerable, white-bearded El. In Daniel's vision, the second heavenly figure, the rider on the clouds, is most plausibly identified as the archangel Michael, who is introduced as "the prince of Israel" later in the book (Daniel 10:13). Canaanite mythology is thus transformed; it is not entirely dead.[6] In later Jewish tradition, this text

---

*Some ancient interpreters read this text so that the "Ancient One" and "the one like a son of man" are one and the same. This reading is found in some manuscripts of the Greek Bible, but it is incompatible with the Masoretic text.

from Daniel proved controversial because it provided a basis for the idea that there are "two powers in heaven."[7] The rabbis rejected this idea as heretical, but nonetheless it was evidently held by some Jews—as well as by Christians.

The "one like a son of man" in Daniel is what we might call a super-angel. This kind of figure appears quite regularly in Jewish texts around the turn of the era.[8] Consider the following passage from Psalm 82 in the fragmentary Melchizedek scroll from Qumran Cave 11: "*Elohim* [God] has taken his place in the divine council; in the midst of the gods he holds judgment." The scroll then provides a gloss on the quoted passage: "Its interpretation concerns Belial and the spirits of his lot [who] rebelled by turning away from the precepts of God ... and Melchizedek will avenge the vengeance of the judgments of God."[9] The *elohim* who rises for judgment in the divine council is here identified as Melchizedek

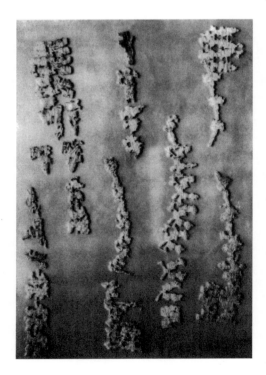

The Melchizedek Scroll, consisting of 13 Dead Sea Scroll fragments found in Qumran's Cave 11, contains a passage from Psalm 82: "Elohim has taken his place in the divine council; in the midst of the gods he holds judgment." The scroll tells us that Elohim ("god" in Hebrew) is Melchizedek, who is also identified as the archangel Michael; Melchizedek presides over the judgment of his demonic counterpart, the Prince of Darkness.

(the identification is probably even more explicit in a later, fragmentary, passage). Another text, the Testament of Amram, tells us that Melchizedek was one of the names for an angel who was also known as Michael and the Prince of Light; this good angel was paired with the evil angel Melchiresha, also known as Belial or the Prince of Darkness.[10] Both Michael and the Prince of Light appear in other Qumran scrolls, most notably the War Scroll. What is striking about Melchizedek in the Cave 11 text is that he is identified as an *elohim*, a god. But, in fact, this usage is not exceptional. The great Jewish scholar Yigael Yadin pointed out 40 years ago that the beings we call angels are called *elim*, gods, in the War Scroll,[11] and the same usage can be found in the Songs of Sabbath Sacrifice, an early mystical text also found at Qumran.[12]

Given the appearance of such semidivine figures in Jewish texts, the term "monotheism" is not entirely felicitous as a description of Jewish beliefs in this pre-Christian period. Yet it is not entirely inappropriate either. These texts always distinguish clearly between the supreme God and his angelic lieutenant. In the Qumran War Scroll, for example, a passage about the Prince of Light is quickly followed by a question addressed to God: "Which angel or prince can compare with thy succor?" (column 12). It is also true that these principal angels are not usually worshiped, but the issue of worship is not as straightforward as is sometimes supposed. The "one like a son of man" in Daniel is given dominion and glory and kingship, and all peoples serve him. Whether this constitutes worship would seem to be a matter of definition.

The "one like a son of man" underwent some development in Jewish tradition, quite apart from the adaptation of this imagery in Christianity.[13] In the Similitudes of Enoch,* a work of uncertain, but clearly Jewish, origin and probably dating to the first century C.E., the visionary sees "one who had a head of days, and his head

---

*Chapters 37-71 of 1 Enoch are called the Similitudes or "parables" of Enoch.

was white like wool, and with him there was another whose face had the appearance of a man and his face was full of grace, like one of the holy angels" (1 Enoch 46:1). The latter figure is subsequently referred to as "that Son of Man." It is said of this figure that "his name was named" before the sun and the stars. He is hidden with God, only to be revealed at the Judgment. Later, in the Judgment scene, this figure is, like God, set on a throne of glory, and the kings of the earth are commanded to acknowledge him (1 Enoch 60-62). Finally, at the end of the Similitudes, Enoch is lifted aloft into the presence of that Son of Man; he is then greeted by an angel, who tells him, "you are the Son of Man who is born to righteousness" (1 Enoch 71:14). Whether this means that Enoch himself is identified with the same Son of Man he had seen in his visions is disputed. The passage can also be translated as "you are a son of man [that is, a human being] who has righteousness." It is also possible that this passage is a later addition to the text, intended to counter the Christian claim that Jesus was the Son of Man by identifying this figure with the Jewish prophet Enoch. In any case, this non-Christian Jewish text provides an intriguing example of the exaltation of a human being to the heavenly realm.

This tradition of the super-angel reached a climax several centuries later, in another Jewish text known as 3 Enoch or *Seper Hekalot*.[14] A figure known as Metatron, Prince of the Divine Presence, is "called by the name of the Creator with seventy names ... [and is] greater than all the princes, more exalted than all the angels, more beloved than all the ministers, more honored than all the hosts and elevated over all potentates in sovereignty, greatness and glory" (3 Enoch 4:1). Metatron is given a throne like the throne of glory (3 Enoch 10:1) and is even called "the lesser YHWH" (3 Enoch 12:5). When Aḥēr, one of the four sages reputed to have ascended to Paradise in the early second century C.E., sees Metatron seated as a king with ministering angels beside him as servants, Aḥēr declares, "There are indeed two powers in heaven!" (3 Enoch 16:3). Because of this, we are told, Metatron is dethroned and given 60 lashes of fire.

Metatron's punishment suggests that there was some controversy about his exalted status at the time 3 Enoch was written. But the tradition that he had a throne in heaven could not be suppressed entirely. Metatron is still identified with Enoch, son of Jared, who was taken up to heaven before the Flood (see Genesis 5:24). Evidently, Metatron is a later development of the Son of Man figure in the Similitudes of Enoch, and has attained an even more exalted rank in the intervening centuries.

Exalted human beings. The case of Enoch brings us to a second kind of divine being under the Most High God: the exalted human being. In Daniel 12, the righteous martyrs of the Maccabean era are promised that they will shine like the brightness of the firmament and be like the stars forever and ever. In 1 Enoch 104, this imagery is clarified: "You will shine like the lights of heaven ... and the gate of heaven will be opened to you ... for you will have great joy like the angels of heaven ... for you will be companions to the host of heaven."

In the idiom of apocalyptic literature, the stars are the angelic host. When the righteous dead become like the stars, they become like the angels; in the Hellenistic world, to become a star was to become a god. We find a reflection of this way of thinking in a Jewish wisdom text attributed to the Greek gnomic poet Phocylides. The author expresses the hope "that the remains of the departed will soon come to the light again out of the earth, and afterwards become gods."[15] This does not mean, of course, that the righteous dead are on a par with the Most High God (or with the Olympian gods) or that worship should be directed toward them (although the dead have been worshiped in many cultures). But it does indicate that the line separating the divine from the human in ancient Judaism was not as absolute as is sometimes supposed.

Some exalted human beings were more important than

others. In the second century B.C.E., an Alexandrian Jew named
Ezekiel wrote a Greek tragedy about the Exodus. In the play,
Moses has a dream:

> I dreamt there was on the summit of Mt. Sinai
> a certain great throne extending up to heaven's cleft,
> on which there sat a certain noble man
> wearing a crown and holding a great scepter
> in his left hand. With his right hand
> He beckoned to me, and I stood before the throne.
> He gave me the scepter and told me to sit
> on the great throne. He gave me the royal crown,
> and he himself left the throne.
> I beheld the entire circled earth
> both beneath the earth and above the heaven,
> and a host of stars fell on its knees before me;
> I numbered them all,
> They passed before me like a squadron of soldiers.
> Then seized with fear, I rose from my sleep.[16]

The figure on Mt. Sinai who vacates his throne for Moses can only
be God. If Moses sits on God's throne, then he is in some sense
conceived of as divine. While the dream is part of a literary work,
there can be little doubt that it reflects wider traditions about
Moses. These traditions are also apparent in the *Life of Moses* by
the first-century C.E. philosopher Philo, also an Alexandrian Jew.
In Exodus 7:1, God tells Moses: "I have made you a god to
Pharaoh." Philo correspondingly writes that "Moses was named
god and king of the whole nation" (*Life of Moses* 1.55-58).[17] It has
been suggested that "god" in this passage is an allegorical equiva-
lent for "king,"[18] but the choice of the term "god" can hardly be
incidental. While Philo insisted that "He that is truly God is one,"
he also recognized other divine entities, such as the Logos, that
existed under God.

Another case of qualified divinization concerns the Davidic

messiah. The notion that the Davidic king was the son of God is well established in the Hebrew Bible in 2 Samuel 7:14 and in Psalm 2:7. It was only natural then that the coming messianic king should also be regarded as the Son of God. The Florilegium from Qumran (4Q174) explicitly interprets 2 Samuel 7:14 in a future, messianic, sense: "I will be a father to him and he will be a son to me. He is the Branch of David, who will arise ... at the end of days." A fragmentary Aramaic text (4Q246), popularly known as "The Son of God Text," predicts the coming of a figure who will be called "Son of God" and "Son of the Most High"; this figure is probably the Davidic messiah, though some scholars dispute this interpretation.[19] To say that the king was the son of God, however, does not necessarily imply divinization. Israel, collectively, is called God's son in the Book of Exodus and again in Hosea, and the "righteous man" is identified as God's son in the Wisdom of Solomon, a first-century C.E. Jewish text from Alexandria. There are other traditions, however, that suggest a more exalted status for the messianic king.

Rabbi Akiba is said to have explained the plural "thrones" in Daniel 7:9 as "one for God, one for David."[20] In the Psalms, traditionally attributed to David, there seems to be a clear scriptural warrant for the enthronement of the messiah: "The Lord said to my Lord, sit at my right hand" (Psalm 110:1). In fact, however, the first messianic interpretation of this text is found in the New Testament (Mark 12:35-37; Acts 2:34-36). In the Similitudes of Enoch, the Son of Man figure is also called "messiah," although he does not appear to have an earthly career. Another Jewish apocalypse, 4 Ezra, written at the end of the first century C.E., interprets Daniel's "son of man" vision in terms of a figure who rises from the sea on a cloud, takes his stand on a mountain and defeats the Gentiles in the manner of the Davidic messiah. This figure is also called "my son" by God. The Similitudes and 4 Ezra are witnesses of a tendency to conceive of a quasi-divine messiah in Jewish texts of the first century C.E.

A final example of exalted humanity involves a very fragmentary text from Qumran (4Q491), in which the speaker claims to have "a mighty throne in the congregation of the gods" and to have been "reckoned with the gods (*elim*)."[21] We cannot be sure who the speaker is supposed to be; suggestions have ranged from the Teacher of Righteousness* to some later sectarian teacher to the messianic High Priest. It does seem clear, however, that the speaker is not an angel or other heavenly creature but an exalted human being. It is not unusual in hymns from Qumran for the hymnist to claim that he enjoys the fellowship of the heavenly host, but this text seems to claim a higher degree of exaltation. Once again, we find that a human being could be reckoned among the *elim* or gods. Even in a conservative Jewish community like Qumran, such an idea was not taboo.

Wisdom and Logos. Our third category of quasi-divine being or entity is the personification of Wisdom, who was identified with the Greek philosophical concept of Logos (Word or Reason) in the Hellenistic period. According to Proverb 8:22, "God created [the female figure Wisdom] at the beginning of his work, the first of his acts of long ago," and she then accompanied him in the creation of the world. In the Book of Ben Sira, written in the early second century B.C.E., Wisdom increasingly resembles the Creator: "I came forth from the mouth of the Most High, and covered the earth like a mist. I dwelt in the highest heavens, and my throne was in a pillar of cloud. Alone I compassed the vault of heaven and traversed the depths of the abyss" (Ben Sira 24:3-5). According to the Wisdom of Solomon, written around the turn of the era in Alexandria, Wisdom brought Israel out of Egypt and holds all things together. Ben Sira's statement that Wisdom came forth from the mouth of the Most High already hints at the

*The Teacher of Righteousness is believed by many scholars to have been the leader of the Qumran community that produced the Dead Sea Scrolls.

identification of Wisdom with Word, which is made explicit in the Wisdom of Solomon.

The Word, or Logos, had another set of connotations in Greek philosophy. The Stoics conceived of the Logos as an immanent god—the principle of rationality in the world—and as a kind of world soul. (It can also be called Spirit or Pneuma, although it is understood as a fine material substance.) The Jewish philosopher Philo adapted this concept of the Logos for a Jewish theology that acknowledged a transcendent creator God.[22] For Philo, the Logos is "the divine reason, the ruler and steersman of all" (*On the Cherubim* 36) and it stands on the border that separates the Creator from the creature (*Who is the Heir* 2-5). But this Logos is also said to be a god. In his *Questions on Genesis*, Philo asks: "Why does [Scripture] say, as if of another God, 'In the image of God He made man' and not 'in His own image'? Most excellently and veraciously this oracle was given by God. For nothing mortal can be made in the likeness of the Most High One and father of the universe, but only in that of the second God, who is His Logos." Here Philo unabashedly calls the Logos a "second God," and this is not the only passage in which he gives the title "God" to the Logos,[23] though he also refers to it as an angel or as God's first-born son.

Does Philo then believe in two Gods? He addresses this question explicitly in his treatise *On Dreams* 1.227-229, where he comments on a passage in the Greek Bible that reads "I am the God who appeared to thee in the place of God" (Genesis 31:13). Philo writes:

> And do not fail to mark the language used, but carefully inquire whether there are two Gods; for we read "I am the God that appeared to thee," not "in my place" but "in the place of God," as though it were another's. What then are we to say? He that is truly God is one, but those that are so called by analogy are more than one. Accordingly the holy word in the pre-

sent instance has indicated Him who truly is God by means of the articles, saying "I am the God," while it omits the article when mentioning him who is so called by analogy, saying "who appeared to thee in the place" not "of the God" but simply "of God."[24]

Philo does not seem to regard the use of "God" as a designation for the Logos as improper,[25] although he clearly distinguishes between the supreme God and the intermediary deity.

So was Judaism monotheistic in the Hellenistic period? The evidence we have reviewed comes from two areas of Judaism, apocalyptic circles in Palestine, including but not limited to the Dead Sea sect, and the Hellenized Alexandrian Judaism of Philo. Not all Jews shared these ideas and beliefs, but they are, nonetheless, indisputably Jewish.

In this literature, the supremacy of the Most High God is never questioned, but there is considerable room for lesser beings who may be called "gods," *theoi* or *elim*. Moreover, both the authors of the apocalyptic literature and Philo single out one preeminent divine or angelic being under God—a super-angel—called by various names in the apocalyptic texts and identified as the Logos by Philo.

It is often said that the practice of monotheism is shown in Jewish worship, which was reserved for the Most High God and did not extend to lesser divinities or angels. It is certainly true that the official sacrificial cult in Jerusalem was monotheistic, and no evidence indicates that any being other than the God of Israel was worshiped in synagogue services. There is some evidence, however, for the veneration of angels.[26] Christian authors such as Clement of Alexandria and Origen claimed that Jews worshiped angels, and both apocalyptic and rabbinic texts prohibit the worship of angels. Presumably, the prohibitions would not have been necessary if the practice had been unknown. There is also some evidence for the practice of calling on angels in prayer, especially in the context of magic. None of this, however, implies that there was an organized, public cult of angels or that the religious authorities sanctioned such activities.

More significant for our purposes is the kind of honor bestowed on the "one like a son of man," in Daniel 7, who is given "dominion and glory and kingship, that all peoples, nations, and languages should serve him" (Daniel 7:14). Similarly, in the Similitudes of Enoch we are told that "all those who dwell on the dry ground will fall down and worship" before that Son of Man (1 Enoch 48:5). The passage continues, however, by stating that they will bless, praise and celebrate with psalms the name of the Lord of Spirits—so there is some doubt as to whether the worship is directed at the Son of Man or the Lord God. According to the "Son of God Text" from Qumran, when war ceases on earth, all cities will pay homage either to the "Son of God" or to "the people of God." Although the homage in this passage involves political submission, worship in the ancient world was often considered analogous to submission to a great king.

Both the "Son of Man" passages and the "Son of God Text" are eschatological: They describe the future; they do not imply that there was any actual cult of either the "Son of Man" or the "Son of God." But they do suggest that some form of veneration or homage could be directed to these figures in the eschatological future.[27] Each of these figures, to be sure, can be understood as God's agent or representative, so that homage given to them is ultimately given to God. But these passages also show that the idea of venerating God's agent, at least in the eschatological future, was not unthinkable in a Jewish context.

Was Christianity Monotheistic?

The veneration of Jesus by his first-century C.E. Jewish followers should be somewhat less surprising in light of the foregoing evidence. Those who believed that Jesus was righteous and unjustly executed would naturally believe that he was exalted to heaven after his death. But more was at issue in the case of Jesus. He was crucified as King of the Jews, which means that he was viewed by the Romans as a messianic pretender and, presumably, by some of his followers as a messianic king. In Luke 24:19, the disciples talk "about Jesus of Nazareth, who was a prophet mighty in deed and word before God and all the people, and how our chief priests and leaders handed him over to be condemned to death and crucified him. But we had hoped that he was the one to redeem Israel." Their bewilderment over Jesus' death is then relieved by the belief that he has risen from the dead.

Whatever the nature of the resurrection experience, it is undeniable that the belief in it arose very shortly after Jesus' death. The resurrection was taken as confirmation that Jesus was indeed the messiah, even though he had not restored the kingdom to Israel, as some had hoped. According to Paul, Jesus was "declared [or appointed?] to be Son of God with power according to the spirit of holiness by resurrection from the dead" (Romans 1:4). Although Jesus had unfinished business as messiah, this anomaly was explained by appeal to Daniel 7: Jesus was the "one like a son of man" who would come again on the clouds of heaven. Like the Similitudes of Enoch, the Gospel of Matthew envisions the Son of Man, Jesus, seated on a throne of glory and presiding over the Last Judgment (see Matthew 25:31). In the Gospels, Jesus is said to have spoken of himself as the Son of Man who would come on the clouds of heaven, but it is more likely that he was so identified by the disciples after his death, when he was no longer present on earth.

According to the Gospel of John, the claim that Jesus was Son of God was blasphemous to his Jewish contemporaries: "We have a law, and according to that law he ought to die because he has claimed to be the Son of God" (John 19:7). Despite this statement, the claim to be the son of God was not inherently blasphemous in a Jewish context. In the Wisdom of Solomon, it is the righteous man who claims to be the child of God and boasts that God is his father (Wisdom of Solomon 2:13,16). To claim to be the son of God, in a Jewish context, was not to claim to be equal to God. Nor was it blasphemous to claim that someone was the messiah, the promised heir to the Davidic line. According to Jewish tradition, the great Rabbi Akiba hailed the revolutionary Simeon Bar Kokhba as the messiah, about a century after Jesus. Rabbi Akiba proved to be mistaken, but he was not deemed a heretic. Some Jews apparently believed that the Son of Man, and later the exalted Metatron, was the human patriarch Enoch exalted to heaven. Even the extreme claim of the Gospel of John that the Word was God could be defended in a Jewish context by appeal to Philo's distinction between the analogical use of "God" without the article, which could refer to the Logos, and "the God," with the article, which was reserved for the Most High (although it is by no means clear that the author of John's gospel intended such a distinction).

Nonetheless, the claim in the Gospel of John that "the Father and I are one" is without parallel in Judaism.[28] By the end of the first century C.E., the exaltation of Jesus had reached a point where it was increasingly difficult to reconcile with Jewish understandings of monotheism.

The apocalyptic understanding of Jesus reaches its New Testament climax in the Book of Revelation. There John sees "one like a Son of Man, clothed with a long robe and with a golden sash across his chest. His head and his hair were white as white wool, white as snow; his eyes were like a flame of fire" (Revelation 1:13-14). The figure in question, Jesus, combines attributes of both the "one like a son of man" and the "Ancient One" of Daniel 7.[29] He has become difficult to distinguish from the God of Israel.[30]

In some part, the tendency to identify Jesus with the God of

Akhenaten and his wife, Nefertity, make offerings to the Sun-disc (the god Aten), in this 3.5-foot-high alabaster carving from Amarna. For the royal couple, the Sun-disc was the sole, universal, self-created Creator. Thus the Egyptian pharaoh Akhenaten (1352-1336 B.C.E.) is often called "the first monotheist."

RICHARD NOWITZ

ZEV RADOVAN

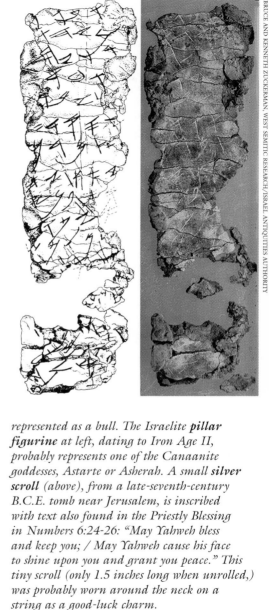

*The mound of Megiddo (opposite) has yielded a number of Israelite cultic objects from Iron Age II (1000-586 B.C.E.)— including small horned altars (see page 34) used for making offerings to the deity. At biblical Dothan, the only known Israelite cultic site from the period of the Judges (12th century B.C.E.), excavator Amihai Mazar found an altar-like installation and a 7-inch-long **bronze bull** (opposite, bottom); this bull suggests that the Israelite god Yahweh may once have been associated with the Canaanite god El, often*

*represented as a bull. The Israelite **pillar figurine** at left, dating to Iron Age II, probably represents one of the Canaanite goddesses, Astarte or Asherah. A small **silver scroll** (above), from a late-seventh-century B.C.E. tomb near Jerusalem, is inscribed with text also found in the Priestly Blessing in Numbers 6:24-26: "May Yahweh bless and keep you; / May Yahweh cause his face to shine upon you and grant you peace." This tiny scroll (only 1.5 inches long when unrolled,) was probably worn around the neck on a string as a good-luck charm.*

ZEV RADOVAN

Taanach cult stand. *This 3-foot-high, terra-cotta stand, from the late-tenth-century B.C.E. Israelite site of Taanach, has four tiers. The second tier from the bottom shows two sphinxes, which may represent the cherubim that adorned the Jerusalem Temple (see 1 Kings 8:6-7). The bottom tier has two lions flanking a female figure—possibly the Canaanite goddess Asherah, who is often described as riding on the back of a lion.*

Israel began with early Christians attempting to claim for Jesus everything that Jews would claim for an intermediary figure.[31] But then it went further; Jesus was the Son of God in a unique sense, and this claim was expressed in Hellenistic idiom in stories of his birth from a virgin. Revelation 12 relates a fragment of a Jewish myth in which the archangel Michael does battle with a dragon in heaven, a variant of a combat myth that was widespread in the ancient Near East. In Revelation, however, we are told that it is by the blood of the Lamb (the crucifixion of Jesus) that the dragon is defeated (Revelation 12:11).[32] Michael fights the battle, but Jesus gains the victory. Similarly, the Epistle to the Hebrews is at pains to insist that Jesus is superior to the angels: "For to which of the angels did God ever say, 'You are my son; today I have begotten you?'" (Hebrews 1:5). Hebrews even applies to Jesus the statement of Psalm 110:4, "you are a priest forever after the order of Melchizedek" (Hebrews 5:6), even though Jesus of Nazareth was not a priest at all. Again, if Hellenistic Judaism venerated the Logos, or Word, as "a second God," the Gospel of John goes one better by claiming that Jesus is the Word and the Word is God.*

This proliferation of honorific titles and claims made on Jesus' behalf by the early Christians goes hand in hand with the veneration, or worship, of Jesus in the early Church. Paul declared that "at the name of Jesus every knee should bend in heaven and on earth and under the earth, and every tongue should confess that Jesus Christ is Lord, to the glory of God the Father" (Philippians 2:10-11). In Revelation, we find the same blessing addressed to the Lamb (Christ) as to "the one seated on the throne" (God): "blessing and honor and glory and might forever

*Since both the Logos and the Danielic son of man were thought to be pre-existent by first-century C.E. Jews (that is, to have been created before the rest of the world), Jesus was believed to be pre-existent, too. In the Gospel of John, the Logos is not said to have been created: It simply was in the beginning. Eventually Christian doctrine would settle on the claim that Jesus was "begotten, not made."

and forever" (Revelation 5:13). Now, Revelation pointedly rejects the worship of angels; and John is rebuked twice for prostrating himself before an angel (Revelation 19:10, 22:9).[33] Yet Christ has many angelic features in Revelation (especially if the "Son of Man" in Revelation 14:14 is identified as Christ).[34] Moreover, the homage paid to Christ in Revelation is reminiscent of the homage paid to the super-angelic Son of Man in Daniel 7: dominion and glory and kingship, so that all peoples, nations and languages should serve him.

The notion that there was a second divine being *under* God was not intrinsically incompatible with Judaism, although the belief that Jesus of Nazareth was such a being undoubtedly seemed preposterous to many Jews. What was incompatible with Judaism was the idea that this second divine being was equal to God. Hence the argument attributed to the Jews in the Gospel of John: According to Jewish law, Jesus ought to die, for he made himself equal to God. Indeed, in the Gospel of John, Jesus is said to claim unabashedly that "the Father and I are one" (John 10:30). Yet this very formulation shows something of the peculiarity of the Christian confession. Jesus is not "a second God" like Philo's Logos; he is one with the Father, so that those who worship both Father and Son can still claim that they worship only one God.

Eventually, Christian theology would be further complicated by the doctrine of the Holy Spirit, which also has its roots in the New Testament and even in pre-Christian Judaism. Over the next few centuries, Christian theologians would labor to find acceptable formulas that would enable them to affirm the divinity of Jesus and the Spirit, but still maintain the unity of God. Along the way, several formulas were rejected as heretical. In the second century C.E., Justin Martyr, following in the footsteps of Philo, spoke of the Logos as "another God" beside the Father; he added that the Logos was other "in number, not in will," and proposed the analogy of one torch lit from another—suggesting different

The Holy Trinity. This detail from Gonzaga Family in Adoration, *by Peter Paul Rubens (1577-1640), presents a typical image of the Christian Trinity. The Father, at right, holds a globe, symbolizing creation; the Son is seated at the right hand of God; and the Holy Ghost, a white dove, flutters between the Father and Son. The notion that a single godhead might have several aspects, each of which could be separately represented, was found both in Hellenistic Judaism and in Christianity.*

manifestations of the same divine entity.[35] This position led to the Monarchian controversy about the unity of God. The Monarchians adopted the position that the Father and Son are one and the same, two aspects of the same being.* A century and a half later, an Alexandrian presbyter named Arius ignited one of the great controversies of Christian antiquity by teaching, in the tradition of Philo, that the Logos was part of the created order and thus was not God in the same sense as the Father. The Council of Nicea,

---

*This position became known as "Patripassianism" (the doctrine that the Father suffers) because it implied that God the Father died on the cross and as "Modalism" because it viewed the Father, Son and Spirit as modes of the same being.

convened by the emperor Constantine in 325 C.E., condemned Arianism as a heresy, and adopted the creed that the Son is "one in being (*homoousious*), with the Father" and that the Spirit "proceeds from the Father and the Son."[36] Even people who signed the decree at the time understood these formulas in different ways, and the controversy continued for several centuries.

In traditional Christian theology, the doctrine of the Trinity is a mystery, which entails an admission that it is not entirely amenable to rational logic and understanding. Non-Christians, and many Christians who lack the appetite for metaphysical reasoning, may be forgiven for thinking that this allows for some equivocation, enabling Christianity to maintain contradictory positions without admitting it. Be that as it may, Christianity has never wavered in its claim to be a monotheistic religion. However the different persons of the Trinity are defined, they are to be understood as falling within the overarching unity of God. The notion that God is three as well as one, however, obviously entails a considerable qualification of monotheism.

Both Judaism and Christianity are committed to monotheism, the belief that ultimately there is only one God. Moreover, the break between Christianity and Judaism, particularly in their understanding of monotheistic doctrines, was not as sharp or complete as is sometimes assumed. The Synoptic Gospels can be reconciled quite easily with Jewish understandings of monotheism. The theology of Justin Martyr and Origen, in second-century C.E. Christianity, is not greatly removed from that of Philo, except that the Logos is now believed to be incarnate in the person of Jesus. This was, to be sure, a considerable difference, but the difference lay in the evaluation of a specific historical person rather than in the theological framework of monotheism or di-theism. Philo, for example, could speak of the patriarchs as *empsychoi nomoi*, or "the laws of God incarnate."[37] Only gradually did the Christian understanding of Christ and the Spirit evolve to the point where it was incompatible with any Jewish understanding of monotheism, and this process was only finalized in the fourth century C.E. Even the Nicene Creed (325 C.E.) begins with the confession, "I believe in one God." Despite the logical anomalies of the Trinity, this confession is still repeated in Christian churches to this day.

AUDIENCE QUESTIONS

Question: Was Akhenaten's sun worship simply a religious reform, or was it also a means of consolidating political power?

Donald B. Redford: It's been suggested that Akhenaten had a hidden agenda when he started out. I'm not quite sure about that. But we do know, from the inscriptional material that's coming to light from Karnak, that Akhenaten's new sun temples had thousands of priests associated with them. Maybe these new priests were simply the old priesthood taken over into the new regime. We know that the revenues of the older temples (which all had landed estates to support them) were now being funneled into the new sun temples. Everyone focused their attention on the new sun temples, worshiping Akhenaten and worshiping the sun. Toward the end of his reign and shortly thereafter, when the country was on the rocks economically, people went back to old temples and found them in ruins. They were completely abandoned; weeds were growing in the courtyards. This situation was easily explained: The gods had turned their backs on Egypt.

Q: In the literature about Akhenaten, there seem to be two main schools, one disparaging and one emphasizing his significance as a precursor of Judaic monotheism. The former suggests that he just worshiped an object, the sun, as opposed to a more abstract being. Those who give Akhenaten more credit refer to the phrase you used earlier about the spirit that dwells in the light of the sun, suggesting that he really did have an abstract concept of a godhead pervasive in the universe.

Redford: Well, I don't think his thought was too abstract. At least, what has survived does not suggest that it was. In fact, he has been called a crass materialist.

Q: Perhaps "abstract" is not the word I want. Did he have either a pantheistic or a universal concept of the deity?

Redford: Universal it was, but not pantheistic. As for the two schools you mentioned, it used to be customary to describe Akhenaten as the mentor of Moses, a Christ-like figure, a martyr, and on and on. This caught the attention of writers of fiction. So we have a number of pieces, right up into the 1950s, that portray him exactly that way. It's unfortunate that this is the one period of Egyptian history that has spawned a secondary and now a tertiary literature. The fictional sources are sometimes consulted as primary evidence, and its hard to get people to go right back to the original texts. If there is a turning against Akhenaten, it is partly a reaction against the romanticism of earlier times.

Q: In Akhenaten's day, Egypt became in effect a world power. Isn't the concept of a universal god more befitting a world power than an individual nation?

Redford: I'll concede that. The Sun-disc is the god of all lands, the creator of all peoples, regardless of race or language. But you can find the roots of that idea already in the earlier theology devoted to Amun [the chief god of the Egyptian pantheon]. So the idea of a universal gód is not entirely new, but Akhenaten certainly does dwell on it.

Q: You indicated that Queen Nefertity may have had more influence

Audience Questions   109

on Akhenaten's ideas than originally thought. Would you elaborate on that?

Redford: Yes, the Nefertity phenomenon. This came as a real shock, considering that Egyptian culture always concentrates on the pharaoh; he's the kingpin of the whole system. So it was surprising to discover that one of Akhenaten's Theban temples was built for the queen alone. She alone is depicted in it doing exactly what her husband does elsewhere, making an offering to the Sun-disc and worshiping the Sun-disc. The king does not appear anywhere in the temple. Also surprising is the fact that Nefertity is depicted twice as often as Akhenaten in these early reliefs. Some scholars believe that this evidence suggests her political importance, or perhaps that she played a real role in the new program. Unfortunately, Nefertity is a completely unknown quantity. We do have a letter to her mother-in-law, Queen Tiye, which gives us some impression of Tiye. But Nefertity, no. We have no correspondence to her or from her. She's a mystery.

Q: To what extent, in your judgment, did Akhenaten's ideas survive? They seem to have been almost an isolated eruption, and then the old ways came back again. But was there a memory of his ideas, however you characterize them?

Redford: I'm not sure that the content of Akhenaten's teaching lived on—only his hegira to Amarna, his death and then the return to normalcy. These things may have survived in Egyptian folklore. Unfortunately, we only have the account of Manetho, a third-century B.C.E. Egyptian priest who wrote down Egyptian history in Greek for the Ptolemaic kings. Manetho almost certainly worked from king lists, of which there were probably many copies in the third century B.C.E., and filled them in with material he collected. At the point where you would expect an account of the Amarna period, Manetho thrusts in an interesting story—one that was much debated in Judeo-Hellenistic polemics. The question was, Do Moses and the Israelites turn up in any ancient Egyptian text? The denigrators of the tradition would say, "No, of course he doesn't." But Manetho attempts to answer "yes"; he trots out a long story, from the reign of a "King Amenophis," that involves sending people off to work in the quarries. So one wonders whether this story preserves a memory also preserved in the Bible. That's a fascinating possibility.

Q: Could you repeat your distinction between one-godism and monotheism?

Redford: I was not making a distinction. I was just trying to get away from the term that is used as the title of this seminar, "monotheism."

Q: Would you agree that the pyramidal structure itself suggests monotheism, which then carries down through the ages?

Redford: Oh I see, the pyramidal structure ...

Q: Because it goes up into ...

Redford: Into an apex. I'm not sure whether it was ever interpreted that way, but the pyramidal form has been linked, probably correctly, to an icon sacred to the sun god—namely the Benben stone. According to records from Heliopolis, the Benben stone contained a depiction of the sun's rays and was worshiped as a sacred fetish. The stone doesn't exist anymore; it's been suggested that it was a meteorite. But it is pictured as pyramidal in shape. It seems somehow to have been tied into the shape used for the mortuary structures we call the pyramids.

Q: Is Psalm 104 the prayer of Akhenaten? And if it is, is this continuity a sign that the [monotheistic] idea was carried on?

Redford: Half of the psalm is, but the other half isn't. One half of the psalm appears to paraphrase passages in the Hymn to the Sun-disc, which was carved on the tomb of Akhenaten's royal secretary, Ay, in Amarna. But it's not a direct translation at all. The rest of the psalm dwells on the heroic, macho aspect of God—and that does not come from Akhenaten's hymn. There's another intriguing example. We have an Amarna letter from the king of Tyre, on the coast of modern Lebanon, to Egypt. In his letter, written in Akkadian, the king quotes a hymn that is a perfect translation of an Egyptian sun hymn. How did this happen? The king of Tyre was probably brought up in the pharaoh's court, as were many of these young kids, these Canaanite village head men. When their dads died, they returned home to take over the reigns of Canaanite towns. Many of them would have come back little Egyptians, speaking Egyptian and able to put into Akkadian the hymns they had heard in the court. These hymns certainly had an oral life after Akhenaten. Other things may have survived in the oral culture as well.

Q: Is there any evidence to support Freud's idea that Moses was an Egyptian?

Redford: The name Moses has been compared with a verbal form *mose*, which occurs in names like Thut*mose*. The formula means simply that god X is born. Interestingly, Egyptian names could be abbreviated by eliminating the theophoric element [the divine name attached to a word], so that you might end up with *mose* as a nickname.

Q: You've spoken of a three-part, or triune, aspect of Egyptian deities. Does the Christian Trinity go back to this triune?

Redford: That's something for a church historian. The triune aspect I spoke of with respect to Egypt comes out of a very interesting hymn to the god Ptah. After lauding Ptah and various other deities, the hymn makes the pointed statement that all gods are three:

Amun; the hidden, the latent power; Re, the sun; and Ptah, the earth. Then it goes on to say that there are cities—Thebes, Heliopolis, Memphis—that abide on earth for all time. The interesting component of this tripartite group is Ptah, the central figure in what we call the Memphite theology. This hymn reads as though it were written by one of the pre-Socratic philosophers; Ptah is made the very essence of the universe and is present whenever rational thought or even the articulation of thought is possible. So Ptah exists within his creation, commanding and willing whatever he wants. The hymn is a fascinating document. But it's more a product of syncretism than of monotheism, it seems to me.

Q: I'd like to ask about the possible influence of the Egyptian one-godness on the broad range of phenomena in Israel. We have Israel coming out of Egypt. I don't know when you date Moses, if there was a Moses—who may have had an Egyptian name, as you point out. Egypt dominated what would be Israel for a long time. We have in the archaeological record artifacts that are often called "Egyptianizing," meaning that they look Egyptian but are not exactly Egyptian. There's Egyptian influence in Judah and Philistia. And it has been pointed out that Psalm 104 is in part a copy of an Egyptian text. Time and again, we see strong Egyptian influence, explicitly, implicitly, textually, archaeologically. All of this suggests that Egyptian one-godness may have had an influence on Israelite one-godness. Is that sensible, or off the wall?

Redford: I wouldn't characterize it either way. But I'd like to point out that Egyptian-looking artifacts found in Iron Age Israel and Judah are often really Phoenician.

William G. Dever: Absolutely correct. That's the point. There's much more Phoenician influence. The Egyptian influence is at one remove, via Phoenicia.

Redford: So Phoenicia was the sieve through which Egyptian stuff arrived in Israel. What amazes me is how *few* of the remains found in the Negev and in Judah were imported from Egypt. As a student studying Egypt, I was taken on [Kathleen] Kenyon's dig at Jerusalem. She had something like 40 squares going, but we found only two amulets that could possibly be of Egyptian origin. Now that's Jerusalem in Iron Age II [1000-586 B.C.E.]. So I think that the Negev and Sinai deserts were a significant barrier to contact. At the very least, there was not the kind of cultural contact that we might have expected. No, I don't see any influence.

Now, there are literary affinities. Part of Psalm 104 derives from the Hymn to the Sun-disc. Proverbs 22:17-23:14 seem to derive from an Egyptian text called the *Wisdom of Amenemope*. There are other passages, too. In the first chapter of 1 Samuel, for instance, Hannah, just before she gives birth, breaks into a paean about how the mighty are brought low and the low exalted, how the sad are happy and the happy are now sad, and how the poor are made rich and the rich made poor. This is straight out of Ipuwer [whose *Admonitions* dates to about the 22nd century B.C.E.]. So you do have themes that seem to have been circulating, almost in the air. But I wonder how direct the contact was.

Q: In your judgment, did Egyptian one-godness influence early Israelite theology?

Redford: Well, if you mean Akhenaten, I don't think it did at all. There is the fact that the traditional monotheism of Moses speaks of one god and Akhenaten makes it clear that he is dealing with a single god. But Egypt in the Iron Age and later, when Israel and Judah were coming into contact with it, was noted for the multiplicity of its deities. Egypt was anything but monotheistic during the Iron Age. Moreover, the monotheism of Akhenaten is so distinct from Yahwism that I wonder why the two are compared. Really, there's very little to Akhenaten's religion. It's been pointed out, for example, that Akhenaten's religion is devoid of ethical content; in Mosaic monotheism, the ethical content is quite extensive. No, I don't see any link.

Dever: There's also too great a time lag—five or six centuries before Israelite monotheism really emerges. So there couldn't have been any very direct connection, perhaps only an oral tradition that remained underground for all those centuries.

Q: Can you give a date to the emergence of Israelite monotheism?

Dever: The archaeological evidence is ambiguous, I think. We can say that these mother-goddess figurines, and all the rest, remained in use through the very end of the monarchy. And it is a fact that there are more of them from the eighth and seventh centuries than from the tenth and ninth centuries.

Q: Does the evidence of these figurines necessarily rule out the existence of a theological strand of monotheism, on the part of an official elite or perhaps even a mainstream Judaism?

Dever: I don't doubt that such a strand existed. My point is simply that there is another stream in the archaeological material that is usually overlooked. I don't mean to disparage the biblical text. But I think we have to deal with the question of literacy: How many people in ancient Israel could read the text that later came to make up the Bible? Very few. Most estimates of literacy in antiquity range from one to two percent. And so we're talking about a literate tradition that did not reflect the actual lives of most people. I'm putting in a plea for the common man, and woman. I've never met them, but I've heard they exist.

Q: On the basis of the biblical text, when do you see Israelite monotheism as emerging?

P. Kyle McCarter, Jr.: The kind of monotheism that is characteristic of the region is the worship of the national god. And that is distinct from the religion of the preceding period, the late Middle Bronze Age through the Late Bronze Age [1750-1200 B.C.E.], during which there were numerous local places of worship. The national god is characteristic of the Iron Age; I see it emerging sometime after the 12th century, though we don't have any texts from this period that make it clear. The standard type of religion in the southern Levant during the Iron Age, perhaps with the exception of the Phoenician coast, was basically monotheistic; but the national god could have hypostatic forms that could become independent quasi-independent.

The interesting question, it seems to me, is when does Yahweh become the national god of Israel? When does Yahwism emerge? One way to approach that question is to ask when the first Yahwistic name appears in Israelite tradition. Who is the first person with a Yahwistic name? I think you'll find that the answer lies in the time of the United Monarchy, as early as Saul. The patriarchs do not have Yahwistic names. In the period of the Judges there are no Yahwistic names. But Saul has a son with a Yahwistic name [Malchishua], as well as a son whose name includes the Canaanite god Baʿal as a theophoric element [Eshbaal].

Q: You talked about national gods. I used to think of that as henotheism: There's a national god who rules us, but other peoples have their own gods. The national god is not a universal God. When did Yahweh become universal?

McCarter: I think you're right. The term "henotheism" fits better with the national god phenomenon. As for your question, When did true monotheism emerge out of the national god phenomenon of Iron Age Yahwism? I think there were two major movements. One was the reform movements [of Hezekiah and Josiah], with the repudiation of the various representations of the deity and the repudiation of local cults. The centralization of worship in Jerusalem put a great emphasis on the oneness, the abstractness of the deity.

Second, with the destruction of Jerusalem, God was separated even from that one place; God was ripped out of a geographic limitation and became increasingly abstract. This concept of the universal God was the great achievement of the priestly synthesis in the sixth century B.C.E. That was the seminal moment in which Jewish monotheism was created, in the sixth century.

John J. Collins: There are probably some other points that you can mark along the way. Clearly, the seventh-century destruction of local cults is one, and the priestly synthesis in the sixth century is another. Something else happens in the Hellenistic period [332-37 B.C.E.]. It's only in the Hellenistic period, I would say, that the question of the existence of other gods is raised.

Q: What about Deutero-Isaiah, written around the mid-sixth century B.C.E.? Doesn't it raise the question of the existence of other gods?

Collins: I don't think Deutero-Isaiah is really questioning their existence. I think it's questioning their power. But let me add one other point. Even down through the Hellenistic period and later, even with the rabbis, you sometimes get the idea that other nations should worship their own gods, and that it is impious of other nations not to worship their own gods. At the same time, in some Hellenistic Jewish literature the strong claim is made that all nations should worship the God of Judaism.

Dever: Now see what my colleagues are all doing. They're talking about the literary tradition. When does monotheism appear in the literary tradition? That's one question. I ask a different question: What about the religious practices of most people? For instance, we speak of Edomite religion as being monotheistic, because we know the name of only one deity, Qos. We don't know the name of any female Edomite deity. But the Edomite shrine at Qitmit contains both male and female figurines. In the popular religion you have something entirely different from what the Bible describes.

Collins: When does the cult of goddesses die out?

Dever: The answer is never. In so-called primitive religions, goddess figurines are still prominent. If you want to see a version of spring fertility rites, I can invite you to the campus of the University of Arizona in March. You will see them there, much as in ancient Canaan.

Q: It's interesting that you have all of these little female goddess figurines, all around the Mediterranean. But it seems to me that women are being systematically squeezed out of the important parts of the system, the parts that have power and status. Frankly, I'm not satisfied with a bunch of little dolls.

Dever: Well, as I've said, the goddess figurines are dangerous, and you have to be careful. I have the heretical opinion that the cult of Asherah was systematically driven underground by the late reform movements in Israel and Judah. And it's clear that the later rabbis didn't quite understand who she had been. It's sort of like the word *mipleṣet* (abominable thing?) that Kyle [McCarter] mentioned; it occurs only once in the Hebrew Bible, and we're not exactly sure what it means. We don't know what it is, but get rid of it! Asherah was almost forgotten until she was rediscovered in texts from Ugarit and in the archaeological evidence. It is an obvious fact that women were marginalized in all of these ancient Levantine societies. The texts were written by men and reflected men's concerns. It would be marvelous if we had a Bible written by women, but we don't. Women are only hinted at. And therefore I think the whole tradition is skewed. I believe that by excavating ancient houses, and understanding the light they shed on domestic religion, we can balance out what one of my colleagues calls the logocentric approach to history. Most of us began as textual scholars. But I have been led more or less to look at material, cultural remains and to give them equal weight. They represent another tradition. It's necessary to understand all of these traditions, not just one.

Redford: One comment that might warm your heart: In the Hellenistic and early Roman periods, one of the most dominant cults in the entire Mediterranean was that of Isis.

Collins: We did attempt revival of domestic religion with the Virgin Mary. But it seems to have "Petered" out.

Q: I tend to connect the rise of national Israelite religion with the prophet Amos and universal religion with prophets like Isaiah and Ezekiel. Can you comment on that?

McCarter: I referred earlier to the political units that emerged after the Iron Age was underway, a bit earlier than Amos or Isaiah. It wasn't until the time of Saul or David (10th century B.C.E.)—at least, according to tradition—that nation-states emerged by unifying several city-states. The subjects of this new, larger political unit would worship a common national god. These nation-states had other characteristics. One of the best examples is language. National dialects arose at the same time. Hebrew, for example, became different from Ammonite, or from Edomite. After the split-up of the Israelite United Monarchy, the same phenomenon occurred; we can point to the differences between the Hebrew dialects of the north [Israel] and south [Judah]. Even the handwriting was different. The point is that these nation-states had various national characteristics, and religion was one of them. In Israel, the prophets also played a role in solidifying the nation. I should say here that in distinguishing between "popular" and "official" religion, we've neglected the prophetic stream, which is preserved in the Bible. Bill [Dever], it's not only an elite group.

Dever: No, I agree with you.

McCarter: One of the remarkable things about the Bible is that it does embrace the loyal and not always so loyal opposition along with the official royal position—and they don't always agree.

Dever: Yes, I couldn't agree more. Between the two extremes that I was positing, you do have the prophetic stream, which has to be characterized separately.

Q: How would you characterize the prophets you mentioned? Is it fair to say that Amos wrote in a national context and that Ezekiel wrote in a universal context?

McCarter: Ezekiel, living during the Babylonian Exile [after 586 B.C.E.], was forced to take a more universal view. Amos is more puzzling. He depicts Yahweh as saying, "I brought Israel out of Egypt, and I brought the Philistines out of Caphtor," as though Yahweh is the god of other nations as well. You'd almost think there's a deliberate element of hyperbole, to make a point about Yahweh's greatness. So, yes, I would agree with you; Amos takes a more or less national view, whereas Ezekiel's view is much broader.

Q: Professor Dever did a very good job of showing that there were female goddess figures that are not mentioned in the Bible. But he then disparages the text by saying, "The Bible doesn't tell us what people were like." Couldn't we say, however, that even in historical terms it was the idealism of the literature that was carried forward? And that this is what matters?

Dever: Literature is not life. It's the result of the creative imagination of a few. It reflects life, of course, real life, but also a kind of life to which few have access. And almost all of our reconstructions of the past have been based on great literary traditions—and to that extent they have excluded the majority of people who ever lived. I'm only trying to put in a plea for those others who have been all but forgotten, except by archaeology. I believe that what they did does matter, and I believe that today we have the means of finding out something about them. One other comment: I am not saying that those women—and the men as well—in the villages of Judah who used these female figurines were not Yahwists. I think they were. They *would* have thought of themselves as Yahwists. This was one aspect of Yahweh's creative activity, as far as they were concerned. In a way, the ancients were more sophisticated than we are.

Q: I was struck by your associating the Holy Spirit with Wisdom, which in turn is connected to femaleness. In Hellenistic literature there's the goddess Athena. And in Jewish literature the figure of Wisdom, *hokma*, is female. Is the Christian Holy Ghost also conceived as female in nature?

Collins: You could make a good case for that historically—though later, in patristic Christian theology, the Spirit wasn't feminine. Still later, in some strands of Christian belief during the Middle Ages, you do get a feminine Spirit.

Q: Where in the Hebrew Bible or the New Testament does the concept of the Holy Spirit emerge?

Collins: Well, you have the spirit of God in the Hebrew Bible from quite an early point, as a mold of God's action. More immediately relevant to the Christian idea of the Spirit, though, is the notion of Wisdom. Wisdom was sometimes identified as the Logos; it was also sometimes called the Pneuma, or Spirit, which was another formulation for the Stoic concept of the Logos—meaning a kind of world soul, or the spirit of God in the world. To a great degree, in both Stoicism and in Hellenistic Judaism, the Spirit and the Logos are the same thing. But in Christianity, Christ is identified with the Logos and the Spirit is understood as a separate entity.

GLOSSARY

amulet A small figure of a god or object worn as a protective charm.

Amun The chief god of the New Kingdom in Egypt; usually represented as a ram or a goose, or as wearing a tall, feathered crown.

aniconism The prohibition against representations of a deity. In its less stringent form, aniconism refers to the practice of using symbolic representations of the deity but not depictions of the deity.

anthropomorphic Having a human form or features.

apostasy The renunciation of a religious faith.

astragali Knuckle bones from various animals, often sheep, used in religious ceremonies.

Aten A variant of the sun god in the early New Kingdom in Egypt, elevated to the status of an exclusive, creator god by Pharaoh Akhenaten; often represented by the Sun-disc extending its rays downward towards earth.

Ba'al The Canaanite storm god, whose consort was the goddess Asherah.

bamot "High places" (singular, *bamah*); large open-air platforms used for cultic rituals such as sacrifices.

Belial A name for the devil found in both the Hebrew Bible and the New Testament.

Bes Egyptian god usually associated with music, the household and especially childbirth; often portrayed as a lion or as a dwarf with a crown of feathers.

Canaanites A Semitic people who inhabited the Levant from about 3000 B.C.E.

chthonic From a Greek word for earth; meaning of the earth, as opposed to of the heavens.

Dead Sea Scrolls Texts and textual fragments in Hebrew, Aramaic and Greek, dating from about 250 B.C.E. to 70 C.E., most of them found in the late 1940s in 11 caves near the town of Qumran, on the northwestern coast of the Dead Sea.

deification The act of making an object or being into a god.

Diaspora Jewish settlements outside the Land of the Bible.

El Chief god of the Canaanite pantheon, often depicted as a bull.

Enoch A son of Cain and the father of Methuselah, according to the Hebrew Bible; traditional author of three visionary pseudepigraphical books.

eschatology The belief that the world, at least in its present form, is about to end—perhaps to be replaced by a new order.

Hathor Ancient Egyptian mother goddess often portrayed as a cow or cow-headed woman with a distinctive horned headdress.

Hellenistic Relating to Greek art, culture or religion after the reign of Alexander the Great, from 332 B.C.E. into the first century B.C.E.

henotheism The belief in one god for one locale or people and other gods for other locales and peoples.

homoousious Literally "of the same substance" in Greek. In the fourth century C.E., Christian homoousians believed that the Son (Jesus) is of the same substance as the Father (God), in accordance with the Nicene Creed.

Horus The Egyptian god of the sky associated with the role of the king; often portrayed as a falcon or a hawk-headed man.

hypostatization The act of attributing tangible form to an abstract idea.

iconography Traditional images or symbols associated with a subject, especially religious or legendary material, such as the use of a book to represent wisdom or knowledge.

in situ Literally "in place"; an archaeological term used to indicate an object's original material context.

Logos The rationality and intelligibility inherent in the universe. The Stoics believed, for example, that the regular motion of heavenly bodies was one manifestation of the Logos.

masseboth Literally "standing stones" (singular, *massebah*); small stone pillars used as altars, or as boundary markers indicating the perimeters of local shrines, or as aniconic representations of a deity.

Melchizedek A priest-king of Jerusalem who prepares a ritual meal for Abraham and receives in return one tenth of the spoils of Abraham's conquests (Genesis 14:18-20).

Metatron Prince of the Divine Light in the Jewish pseudepgraphical text 3 Enoch (fifth-sixth century C.E.); possibly a later development of the Son of Man, mentioned in the Book of Daniel (mid-second century B.C.E.) and in the New Testament.

monad In theology an elemental spiritual substance from which all material properties are derived.

monolatry The restriction of worship to one god without denying the existence of other gods.

naos A small model of a temple, often used as a household shrine (plural, *naoi*).

Nicene Creed A tenet of Christian belief expanded from a creed issued by the first Nicene Council (325 C.E.) concerning the one-fold nature of the Trinity. The Nicene Creed, beginning with the words "I believe in one god," is often used in liturgical worship.

numina Spiritual beings.

onomasticon A list of personal names from a particular time and place.

pithos A large pottery storage vessel (plural, *pithoi*).

pneuma Literally "breath" or "wind"; used in ancient Greek philosophy to refer to the vital spirit or soul.

polydemonism The worship of many spirits or demons.

polytheism The belief in or worship of more than one god.

Qumran A site near the northwest corner of the Dead Sea, roughly 10 miles south of Jericho. The Dead Sea Scrolls were found in caves in a line of hills just above Qumran.

rabbinical Referring to the rabbis' consolidation of the scriptural canon and their commentaries on Jewish legal traditions. The rabbinical period began in the first and second centuries C.E.

Sed Festival A jubilee festival held by Egyptian kings after 30 years of rule and then repeated every three years thereafter. The festival involved, among other activities, a ritual recoronation of the king to confirm his reign.

sherds Fragments of pottery found at archaeological sites.

stela An upright stone or pillar, frequently bearing an inscription or a design or both (plural, stelae).

Stoicism School of philosophy founded by Zeno of Citium, Cyprus, in Athens in the late fourth century B.C.E. According to Zeno's ethical doctrine, the only real good is virtue and the only real evil is moral weakness; nothing else—not poverty, pain or death—has actual existence. A virtuous man possesses the only real good and is, therefore, happy.

syncretism The combination of different forms of belief or practice.

Teacher of Righteousness Believed by many scholars to have been the leader of the community that produced the Dead Sea Scrolls.

terra-cotta Fired clay used for making pottery, statuettes and certain architectural features.

votive Expression of a wish, desire or prayer, generally in reference to a representation of or an offering to a deity.

zoomorphic Having the form of an animal.

List of Illustrations

Akhenaten 13

Egyptian kings of the XVIIIth
and XIXth Dynasties 17

Sobek and Pharaoh
Amenophis III 18

Colossi of Memnon 19

Map of ancient Egypt 21

Temple of Amun in Thebes 22

Akhenaten and the
Sun-disc (detail) 25

Map of ancient Israel 31

Tel Dan "high place" 32

Tel Dan altar 32

Incense shovels from Tel Dan 32

Tel Dan *lishkah* 33

Plan of Tel Dan *lishkah* 33

Megiddo altar 34

Beersheba altar 36

Beersheba 37

Arad "Holy of Holies" 38

Arad altar 38

Bronze lion from Arad 39

Cult stand from Arad 39

Kuntillet ʿAjrud 42

Pithos fragment (and drawing)
from Kuntillet ʿAjrud 43

Inscription (and drawing)
from Khirbet el-Qôm 46

Offering stand from Ai 48

Terra-cotta pillar figurines 51

Terra-cotta ram 51

Shabaka Stone 59

lmlk stamps 61

Pithos fragment from
Kuntillet ʿAjrud 62

Israelite kings of the United
and Divided Monarchies 64

Mary as Wisdom,
by Jan Van Eyck 70

Elephantine papyrus 72

Dead Sea Scroll fragment from
the Book of Deuteronomy 75

Asherah as tree of life (drawing)
from Kuntillet ʿAjrud 78

Daniel's vision of "one like the
son of man" (illumination) 83

Melchizedek Scroll fragment 85

Akhenaten, Nefertity and
the Sun-disc 97

Megiddo 98

Bronze bull from Dothan 98

Silver scroll from Ketef Hinnom 99

Terra-cotta pillar figurine 99

Cult stand from Taanach 100

Gonzaga Family in Adoration
by Peter Paul Rubens 103

ENDNOTES

Folk Religion in Early Israel

[1] On the limitations of the biblical texts and their interaction with archaeology, see William G. Dever, *Recent Archaeological Discoveries and Biblical Research* (Seattle: Univ. of Washington Press, 1990), pp. 3-30; and "'Will the Real Israel Please Stand Up?' Archaeology and Israelite Historiography: Part 1," *Bulletin of the American Schools of Oriental Research (BASOR)* 297 (1995), pp. 61-80.

[2] See Dever, "'Will the Real Israel Please Stand Up?' Part II: Archaeology and the Religions of Ancient Israel," *BASOR* 298 (1995), pp. 37-58, and the literature cited there. A good synthesis and bibliography may be found in Susan Ackerman, *Under Every Green Tree: Popular Religion in Sixth-Century Judah* (Atlanta: Scholars Press, 1992).

[3] See Amihai Mazar, "The 'Bull Site': An Iron Age I Open Cult Place," *BASOR* 247 (1982), pp. 27-42.

[4] See the convenient summary in Avraham Biran, *Biblical Dan* (Jerusalem: Israel Exploration Society, 1994).

[5] Alain Chambon, *Tell el-Far'ah 1: L'Age du fer* (Paris: Éditions Recherche sur les Civilisations, 1984), pl. 66. For other examples of *naoi*, see Saul Weinberg, "A Moabite Shrine Group," *Muse* 12 (1978), pp. 30-48.

[6] Gordon Loud, *Megiddo II: Seasons of 1935-39*, Oriental Institute Publications 62 (Chicago: Univ. of Chicago Press, 1948), pp. 45- 46; figs. 100-102.

[7] See, for example, Ruth Hestrin's "Exploring Semitic Iconography," *Biblical Archaeology Review (BAR)*(September/October, 1991), pp. 57, 58.

[8] Paul W. Lapp, "Taanach by the Waters of Megiddo," *Biblical Archaeologist (BA)* 30 (1967), pp. 2-27. For further discussion of Asherah as the "Lion Lady," see Dever, "Asherah, Consort of Yahweh? New Evidence from Kuntillet 'Ajrûd," *BASOR* 255 (1985), pp. 29-37.

[9] Gabriel Barkay and Amos Kloner, "Jerusalem Tombs from the Days of the First Temple," *BAR*, March/April 1986, pp. 22-39.

[10] See Barkay, "The Priestly Benediction on Silver Plaques from Ketef Hinnom in Jerusalem," *Tel Aviv* 19 (1992), pp. 139-194.

[11] See Yohanan Aharoni, *Beer-Sheba I: Excavations at Tel Beer-Sheba, 1969-71 Seasons* (Tel Aviv: Tel Aviv Univ. Press 1973), pp. 5-67; and Ze'ev Herzog, "Beer-Sheba of the Patriarchs," *BAR*, November/December 1980, pp. 12-28.

[12] See Aharoni, "Arad: Its Inscriptions and Temple" *BA* 31 (1968), pp. 2-32; and for better dating and interpretation, see Herzog et al., "The Israelite Fortress at Arad," *BASOR* 254 (1984), pp. 1-34.

[13] For an early report, see Ze'ev Meshel, "Did Yahweh Have a Consort? The New Religious Inscriptions from Sinai," *BAR*, March/April 1979, pp. 24-34. For drawings, see Pirhiya Beck, "The Drawings from Ḥorvat Teiman (Kuntillet ʿAjrûd)," *Tel Aviv* 9 (1982), pp. 3-86. For a critical review, see Dever, "Asherah, Consort of Yahweh?"

[14] For the original publication, see Dever, "Iron Age Epigraphic Material from the Area of Khirbet el-Kôm," *Hebrew Union College Annual* 40-41 (1970), pp. 139-204. For the considerable literature since then, see the references in Ackerman, "The Queen Mother and the Cult in Ancient Israel," *Journal of Biblical Literature* 112:3 (1993), pp. 391-394.

[15] On offering stands generally, see Mervin D. Fowler, "Excavated Incense Burners," *BA* 47 (1984), pp. 183-186; and LaMoine F. DeVries, "Cult Stands: A Bewildering Variety of Shapes and Sizes," *BAR*, July/August 1987, pp. 26-37. For the connection of Asherah with tree-symbols, see the penetrating works of Ruth Hestrin, "The Lachish Ewer and the 'Asherah,'" *Israel Exploration Journal* 37 (1987), pp. 212-223; and "Understanding Asherah—Exploring Semitic Iconography," *BAR*, September/October 1991, pp. 50-59.

[16] For the Ai stand, still not properly published, see Joseph A. Callaway, "Ai," in *The New Encyclopedia of Archaeological Excavations in the Holy Land*, ed. Ephraim Stern (New York: Simon & Schuster, 1993), vol. 1, p. 45.

[17] See Aharoni, "The Horned Altar of Beer-sheba," *BA* 37 (1974), pp. 2-6.

[18] See Chambon, *Tell el-Farʿah I*; and Weinberg, "A Moabite Shrine."

[19] There exists in English no full-scale study of *kernoi*, but see provisionally Mazar, *Excavations at Tell Qasile, Part 1, The Philistine Sanctuary: Architecture and Cult Objects* (Jerusalem: The Hebrew Univ. of Jerusalem, 1980), pp. 96-98.

[20] For a general discussion of the horses and riders, see J. Glen Taylor, *Yahweh and the Sun: Biblical and Archaeological Evidence for Sun Worship in Ancient Israel*, JSOT Supplement Series 111 (Sheffield, UK: Sheffield Academic Press, 1993), pp. 58-66.

[21] We lack an up-to-date, comprehensive study of the figurines, but in English see Carol Meyers, "Of Drums and Damsels: Women's Performance in Ancient Israel," *BA* 54 (1991), pp. 16-27.

[22] On aspects of "women's cults" in ancient Israel, see Dever, "'Will the Real Israel Please Stand Up? Part 2'"; and Ackerman, *Under Every Green Tree*. Also see Jacques Berlinerblau, *The Vow and the "Popular Religious Groups" of Ancient Israel* (Sheffield, UK: Sheffield Academic Press, 1996).

[23] A number of recent studies have discussed this subject, but none in my opinion even offers a working definition. The list includes Susan Ackerman's *Under Every Green Tree* and Karel van der Toorn's *From Her Cradle to Her Grave: The Role of Religion in the Life of the Israelite and the Babylonian Woman*, JSOT Supplemental Series 164 (Sheffield, UK: Sheffield Academic Press, 1994).

[24] By reading the Hebrew Bible "between the lines" or "against the grain," I do not mean to endorse the deconstructionist method of "standing the text on its head." See Dever, "What Did the Biblical Writers Know, and When Did They Know It?" in the *Festschrift* for Ernest Frehrichs.

[25] See Dever, "The Silence of the Text: An Archaeological Commentary on 2 Kings

23," in *Scripture and Other Artifacts: Essays on the Bible and Archaeology in Honor of Philip J. King*, ed. Michael D. Coogan, J. Cheryl Exum, and Lawrence E. Stager (Louisville, KY: Westminster John Knox Press, 1994), pp. 143-168.

²⁶ The literature on monotheism in ancient Israel is vast. For a recent treatment with bibliography, see Ackerman, *Under Every Green Tree*; see also Bernhard Lang, *Monotheism and the Prophetic Minority* (Sheffield, UK: Sheffield Academic Press, 1983); and Mark S. Smith, *The Early History of God: Yahweh and the Other Deities in Ancient Israel* (San Francisco: Harper & Row, 1990).

²⁷ On the Kabbalah, the works of Gershon Scholem are definitive; see his *Major Trends in Jewish Mysticism* (New York: Schocken Books, 1995).

The Religious Reforms of Hezekiah and Josiah

¹ In Mesopotamia, the Assyrian king Assurbanipal (668-627 B.C.E.) was the chief proponent of neoclassicism. We have copies of his written instructions to his officials, in which he tells them to scour the countryside of Assyria and Babylonia, pore through local temple archives and copy important documents for the royal collection. Since the discovery of Assurbanipal's library in the mid-19th century at ancient Nineveh, in northern Iraq, it has remained our most important source for the "canonical" literature of ancient Mesopotamia.

² Murial Lichtheim, *Ancient Egyptian Literature,* vol. 1 (Berkely and Los Angeles: Univ. of California Press, 1975), p. 52.

³ Frank Moore Cross, *Canaanite Myth and Hebrew Epic* (Cambridge, MA: Harvard Univ. Press, 1973).

⁴ David Ussishkin's excavation of Lachish clarified the previously muddled stratigraphic picture of Judahite sites in the last 150 years before the destruction of Jerusalem in 586 B.C.E., showing that all the *lmlk* jar handles derive from the time of Hezekiah. The exact function of these royal stamps, of which more than 1,200 on handles or whole vessels are now known, is still disputed; but it is clear that they had some kind of national administrative purpose, most probably having to do with preparations for Sennacherib's 701 B.C.E. invasion. All of the *lmlk* inscriptions were made before that invasion, and there is compelling evidence to suggest that they had a central place of manufacture.

⁵ Roland de Vaux, "Táman, ville ou région d'Èdom?" *Revue Biblique* 76 (1969), pp. 379-385.

⁶ See William L. Moran, "The Ancient Near Eastern Background of the Love of God in Deuteronomy," *Catholic Biblical Quarterly* 25 (1963), pp. 77-87.

⁷ Perhaps *mipleṣet* is a cacophemism for *mĕpaleṣṣet*, which means "plane, sculptor's chisel" and possibly, like *pĕsîl* (*Berakot* 4:8a, *Pirke d'Rabbi Eliezer* 30), "hewn image" (cf. Aramaic *miplaṣṭā',* "sculptor's work, engraving").

Jewish Monotheism and Christian Theology

¹ James D.G. Dunn, *The Partings of the Ways Between Christianity and Judaism and Their Significance for the Character of Christianity* (Philadelphia: Trinity Press International, 1991), pp. 19-21.

[2] P. Maurice Casey, *From Jewish Prophet to Gentile God: The Origins and Development of New Testament Christology* (Louisville, KY: Westminster John Knox, 1991), p. 159.

[3] Compare Larry W. Hurtado, *One God, One Lord, Early Christian Devotion and Ancient Jewish Monotheism* (Philadelphia: Fortress, 1988). In his review of this material, Hurtado distinguishes "personified divine attributes" (including Wisdom), exalted patriarchs and principal angels. See also Casey, *From Jewish Prophet to Gentile God*, pp. 78-96; Dunn, *Christology in the Making* (Philadelphia: Westminster, 1980); and Martin Hengel, *The Son of God* (Philadelphia: Fortress, 1976).

[4] Dunn, *Christology in the Making*, p. 74; Casey, *Son of Man: The Interpretation and Influence of Daniel 7* (London: SPCK, 1979), pp. 7-50.

[5] For a full discussion, see John J. Collins, *Daniel*, Hermeneia (Minneapolis: Fortress, 1993), pp. 304-310.

[6] On the continuity between angels and pagan gods, see Paula Hayman, "Monotheism— A Misused Word in Jewish Studies?" *Journal of Jewish Studies* 42 (1991), pp. 1-15.

[7] Alan F. Segal, *Two Powers in Heaven* (Leiden: Brill, 1977), p. 36.

[8] Christopher Rowland, *The Open Heaven* (New York: Crossroad, 1982), pp. 94-113.

[9] See Paul J. Kobelski, *Melchizedek and Melchireša* (Washington: Catholic Biblical Association, 1981), pp. 3-23.

[10] Kobelski, *Melchizedek*, pp. 24-36.

[11] Yigael Yadin, *The Scroll of the War of the Sons of Light Against the Sons of Darkness* (Oxford: Oxford University Press, 1962), p. 230.

[12] Carol A. Newsom, *Songs of the Sabbath Sacrifice: A Critical Edition* (Atlanta: Scholars Press, 1985), p. 23.

[13] Collins, "The Son of Man in First Century Judaism," *New Testament Studies* 38 (1992), pp. 448-466.

[14] See Philip Alexander, "3 (Hebrew Apocalypse of) Enoch," in *The Old Testament Pseudepigrapha* ed. James H. Charlesworth, 2 vols. (New York: Doubleday, 1983), vol. 1, pp. 223-315.

[15] Pieter W. van der Horst, *The Sentences of Pseudo-Phocylides* (Leiden: Brill, 1978), p. 185.

[16] Carl R. Holladay, *Fragments from Hellenistic-Jewish Authors*, vol. 2, *Poets* (Atlanta: Scholars Press, 1989), pp. 363-365.

[17] Wayne A. Meeks, "Moses as God and King," in *Religions in Antiquity*, ed. Jacob Neusner (Leiden: Brill, 1968), pp. 354-371.

[18] Holladay, *Theios Aner in Hellenistic Judaism* (Missoula, MT: Scholars Press, 1977), p. 125.

[19] See Collins, *The Scepter and the Star* (New York: Doubleday, 1995), pp. 154-172.

[20] *Hagiga* 14a; *Sanhedrin* 38b.

[21] Collins, *The Scepter and the Star*, pp. 136-153.

[22] David Winston, *Logos and Mystical Theology in Philo and Alexandria* (Cincinnati: Hebrew Union College Press, 1985).

[23] Compare with *Som* 1.230-233; see also Segal, *Two Powers in Heaven*, p. 163.

[24] Segal, *Two Powers in Heaven*, p. 159. The Hebrew text has "I am the god Bethel" (usually translated "the god of Bethel").

[25] Francis Henry Colson, in the Loeb Classical Library, translates the phrase *en*

katachrēsei as "improper," but the reference is clearly to analogical usage.

[26] Hurtado, *One God, One Lord*, pp. 28-34; Hayman, "Monotheism—A Misused Word in Jewish Studies?" pp. 6-7.

[27] The significance of eschatological figures in this context is noted by P.A. Rainbow, "Jewish Monotheism as the Matrix for New Testament Christology: A Review Article," *Novum Testamentum* 33 (1991), p. 88. The failure to note the new context created by eschatology is a flaw in Hurtado's otherwise excellent book.

[28] The conclusion of Marinus de Jonge ("Monotheism and Christology," in *Early Christian Thought in its Jewish Context*, ed. John Barclay and John Sweet [Cambridge, UK: Cambridge University Press, 1996]) that Jesus' relationship to the Father in the Gospel of John "did not in any way lead to his deification" is difficult to justify.

[29] See Adela Yarbro Collins, "The 'Son of Man' Tradition in the Book of Revelation," *The Messiah*, ed. Charlesworth (Minneapolis: Fortress, 1992), pp. 536-568.

[30] In Revelation 14:14, however, "one like a Son of Man" appears as one in a series of angels. Whether the "Son of Man" in this passage should be identified as Jesus is unclear.

[31] For a fuller account see Dunn, *The Parting of the Ways*, pp. 183-229.

[32] See Adela Yarbro Collins, *The Combat Myth in the Book of Revelation* (Missoula, MT: Scholars Press, 1976), pp. 101-114.

[33] Richard Bauckham, *The Climax of Prophecy. Studies on the Book of Revelation* (Edinburgh: Clark, 1993) pp. 118-149.

[34] Jesus appears as a seventh figure with six angels in Hermas, *Similitudes* 13:6-9 (mid-second century C.E.), in such a way as to suggest that he is the principal of the seven archangels.

[35] Henry Chadwick, *The Early Church* (Harmondsworth, UK: Penguin, 1967), pp. 85-86.

[36] For a summary of the controversies and for illustrative texts, see William G. Rusch, *The Trinitarian Controversy* (Philadelphia: Fortress, 1980); and Richard A. Norris, *The Christological Controversy* (Philadelphia: Fortress, 1980).

[37] Erwin R. Goodenough, *By Light, Light: The Mystic Gospel of Hellenistic Judaism* (New Haven: Yale, 1935), pp. 121-234.

ACKNOWLEDGMENTS

The Biblical Archaeology Society would like to thank the people who made this book possible. Lisa Josephson Straus and Jennifer Cunningham typed and transcribed the manuscripts. Molly Dewsnap copy-edited the book and suggested, among other things, the need for a glossary, which we include at the end. Bridget Young insisted that all phases of the production schedule be punctiliously met. Sean Kennedy's elegant designs grace the book's every page, as well as its cover. And Allison Dickens spent countless hours tracking down and researching the pictures, checking facts and proofreading the manuscripts.